PURPLE FURY

RUMBLING WITH THE WARRIORS

Rob Ryder

Copyright © 2023 by Rob Ryder
All rights reserved. No parts of this publication may be reproduced, distributed, or transmitted in any form or by any means, including photocopying, recording, or other electronic or mechanical methods without the prior written permission of the publisher.
ISBN: 979-8-9892693-1-0

www.purplefury.net

Making movies is a lot like life – a swirling chaotic clusterfuck. So, if you're looking for a polished story that stays on track, clips along in perfect chronological order and rolls into the last station all tied up in a shiny pink bow, you caught the wrong train.

1

You know when you take a new job and three days in you reach that moment of – what the fuck have I done?

The Warriors went like that for me. Until I learned to just roll with it. Follow the flow. Whatever the fuck happens. Follow the flow.

It's 6:30 am as I head into the Gulf & Western Building on Columbus Circle and take an elevator up to the production office.

The place is buzzing. A dozen people working the phones, helping wardrobe, taking calls from casting, writing memos, making copies, ordering bagels, every single freaking thing that needs to be done to get this movie made.

I search out my immediate bosses in the locations office – Alex Ho and David Streit, but they're not there. And I have no idea where they are, or what they want from me today, and I have no way of reaching them. As for them, when you're out of the office, all you've got are pay phones in the streets – if they're working. And that's it. No cell phones. No Zoom. No email. No Facetime. No Snapchat.

In 1978, we are just one step above tin cans and string. We communicate either landline to landline or person to person. Or my baby wrote me a letter.

I grab a bagel and consider my next step. Crew members start straggling in from the night's shoot. Subdued, haggard. Needing to file production reports, write out the new call sheet, address all sorts of other shit for the next night's shoot before they can grind home and crash for a few hours.

Then the 1st Assistant Director walks in, looking like Who Shot Sally. Walter Hill fired him two days ago, but the new A.D. hasn't flown in from Hollywood yet, so this poor soul has lame duck written all over him. The firing wasn't personal, it's just that Walter couldn't stand the guy. Yet here he still is – gritting out his last two days. Being a professional. Dead man walking.

I need to talk to the Production Manager – John Starke. I look across the room to his office – the Production Coordinator at her desk just outside, swamped with people needing Starke's attention.

Starke is good. He's sharp. He's young, but he knows how shit gets done. I'd worked with him two years earlier, my first movie job – a gangster indie with Joe Pesci called *The Bottom Line* or *The Death Collector*, or some other shit title depending on the foreign market. It was made for like half a million bucks, part of a tax write-off scheme, and it's where I cut my movie production teeth.

My gums are still bleeding.

I cross the production office, smile at the coordinator, stand on my tiptoes and grab Starke's attention. Starke hired me onto *The Warriors* as a production assistant – 50 bucks a day – then immediately bumped me up to location scout – 50 bucks a day.

Starke waves me in, and phone still to his ear, goes straight into it, "Hey, okay, Rob, so listen, we need a street that looks inhabited, you know, apartments and shit, storefronts, people living there, where we can blow up a car."

"Blow up a car?"

Starke shoots me a look. "You read the script, right?"

I snap to, "Yeah. I read the script."

"So the scene where they blow up the car. You need to find that street."

"Okay."

"You gotta buy the whole block, right? You gotta find a street where they're gonna let us blow up a car in the middle of the night, and all the neighbors will be cool with it."

"You thinking Queens?"

"Try Brooklyn. There's a van for you downstairs."

"Uh…"

But Starke waves me off to face the shitstorm of other problems heading his way.

It's a long elevator ride to the street. Fuck. I am fucked. I am way over my head with this one. Buy an entire city block in Brooklyn.

I walk through the lobby, spot the van and groan. Because on a union shoot, every vehicle is driven by a Teamster. My first day on *The Warriors* I opened the front passenger door of a van, stuck out my hand to the Teamster behind the wheel and said, "Hi. I'm Rob Ryder."

His reply – "So what?"

Today I slide open the rear door and step in. No more of that – "Front seat, gee whiz, let's ride alongside the Teamster and make nice" for me. Nope. You learn fast working on a movie. Don't try to be friends. Just do your job.

"Where to, pal?"

This driver is new to me. "Brooklyn."

He adjusts his mirror to catch my eye. "Where in Brooklyn?"

I stare at him with a blank look.

"Okay," he shrugs. "Somewhere in Brooklyn."

The van pulls out, the Teamster deciding a run down Broadway is the quickest route to the Brooklyn Bridge (no GPS). I'm muttering in the back seat, fuck, I am beyond fucked. Where do I even start with this one? My vibration is so intense the Teamster picks up on it. As we cross 42nd Street, he again catches my eye in the rearview.

"So, yo, buddy, what's up?"

Wait what? I'm shocked. Did I actually catch a ride with an empathetic Teamster? Maybe I'm not so fucked after all.

I tell him, "I am fucked. I am really fucked."

He says to me, "So what's the actual problem? Every problem has a solution, some better than others maybe, but hey... every problem has a solution."

So, I explain to him that I need to find an entire city block that we can lock down for 24 hours so we can blow up a car in the middle of the night and nobody's gonna have a problem with that – as in, the people who live there.

His response, "Man, you are really fucked."

2

New York City is an amazing, magical place. Nowadays. As it was way back in the 1930s when my parents met on a blind date in a dance hall in Brooklyn. But between then and now, not so much.

It's never been easy to be poor in New York – but my dad brought some imagination to date night. Back then you could ride the Staten Island Ferry for a nickel then catch Billie Holiday in a jazz joint for the price of a beer. Now that is true romance on a budget.

(The heftiest price was bringing my mom home to her strict Polish parents after midnight.)

But New York City in between the 1930s and today? Like the summer of 1978 when *The Warriors* rumbled through town? Things were dark back then. The city was a hard place. Edgy. Mean. Lines running out the doors of unemployment offices, down sidewalks filled with garbage and dog shit. Distrust in every face.

I'd moved to New York a couple years earlier, determined to be a writer, knowing that chasing after doe-eyed girls through fields of wildflowers in the Colorado Rockies wasn't gonna get it done. Nope. Time to leave that hippie carpenter lifestyle behind. If I was gonna be a writer, I needed to suffer. I needed New York.

There was a mentally ill homeless woman who hung out near the entrance to the Lexington Avenue line on East 86th Street. She'd squat in a doorway all day – her face streaked with grime, red hair matted. Blank eyes in a desperate face. My pal Dominic and I would give her a dollar once in a while – gingerly, because she stank and scratched like she had lice.

She was there month after month. Then one day, as she took our meager dollar, we freaked. Because she was visibly pregnant – her round belly straining against her filthy t-shirt. Three days later she was gone.

That was New York City in 1978.

3

Behind the scenes, making a movie is just one dumpster fire after another. There are so many departments, people. So much that can go wrong. There's wardrobe, casting, makeup, hair, art department, set dressers, assistant directors, accounting, transportation, catering, props, electrical, grip, camera, sound… And then there's locations.

My search for the car explosion street is looking hopeless when I'm pulled onto the Coney Island boardwalk. It's maybe four, five days into the shoot. The two location managers are scrambling to stay ahead of things – you can imagine what a nightmare it was.

I'd just gotten bumped up to locations, and I had no fucking clue what I was doing. *The Warriors* was off to a rocky start. Walter Hill having to fire his 1st Assistant Director, then a problem developing with a key cast member, plus Walter was really pissed that not enough locations were locked down.

We're out on the boardwalk and Walter decides to extend the tracking shot he wants. Alex Ho (location manager) rushes up to me and jams a wad of hundreds in my hand – "Look, here's a thousand in hundreds. You gotta buy the next 8 storefronts beyond the balloon guy."

I take the cash. Ho jams a clipboard full of forms into my other hand. "Give them a hundred bucks each – we need their storefront for the next six hours – and make sure they sign this release."

I'm a little dazed, "But…"

"Just fucking do it! I gotta get to the Bronx."

I walk over to the first storefront. The owner's just rolling up his door – "Hey, yeah so I'm from Paramount and we're shooting a movie here, and I can give you a hundred bucks if we can use your storefront for the next six hours."

The guy looks up and down the boardwalk. Nobody's out yet, just a few dozen crew members laying dolly track, pulling cable. He hesitates.

"Listen, man. The cops are shutting down this whole stretch of the boardwalk, you're not gonna have any customers anyway."

"Yeah, sure." The guy takes the C-note and signs the release.

So does the next guy, and the next guy, and I'm feeling like holy shit, this shit is actually working. Two storefronts left. But by now the word is out. And the last two owners are huddling together as I walk up. One of them says, "Yeah, so we hear you're paying a hundred a store. We want more."

Fuck. Fuck me. Down the boardwalk I can see the camera crew setting up, the cast assembling in their shiny leather vests. Pressure building.

The second guy says, "Yeah, like a hundred fifty."

Fuck, I've only got hundreds. I pull the two last storeowners in tight. "Look, I'll give you each 200 bucks, but you can't say a fuckin' word to those other guys. Agreed?"

Agreed. They sign the releases, we clear the boardwalk, Swan and company do their walk, and Walter gets his shot. As we're wrapping out, a couple of the first store owners suddenly stomp up to me. "You owe us money! Cocksucker! You paid those guys a hundred dollars more!"

"Yeah, well, you signed the release, right? So it's a done deal."

"Yeah, yeah?! We're gonna fucking sue your asses!"

And I think to myself, yeah, right, the owner of Squirt Gun Mania is gonna sue Paramount Pictures, which is owned by Gulf & Western, the biggest energy corporation in the world.

"What can I say?" I shrug. "Sorry. I gotta get to the Bronx."

And after all that hard work, all those early shots in the bright Coney Island sun of the Warriors making plans to travel to the big conclave in the Bronx? All those scenes got shit-canned when Walter Hill decided to open the movie in the dark of night.

4

A lot's been said about the hassles real-life New York street gangs caused us in *The Warriors*. Production security took care of it one way or another. (Don't ask, don't tell.)

In addition to real gang-bangers, the cast and crew were constantly harassed and threatened by all sorts of other whackos, low-lifes, wannabes and outright "ran out of meds" lunatics.

We had security on the set. Cops in uniforms. But also, moonlighting cops, hired on to handle the tricky stuff. Two guys in particular. Big, gristled, middle-aged detectives who'd seen it all and more. I remember them wearing long black raincoats and sensible black shoes.

These two were like Popeye Doyle and Buddy Russo, but ten times tougher. *The French Connection*, remember? A brilliant movie, directed by the brilliant, lunatic director, Billy Friedkin. (A story about Friedkin to come later.)

Anyway, our Popeye and Buddy had a surefire way of handling disruptors. I witnessed it again and again.

We'd be night shooting on some godforsaken wet-down street somewhere in Brooklyn, and even at 3 a.m. we'd draw a crowd of looky-loos, straining against the barricades that protected the set. And there'd always be somebody causing trouble. Heckling the cast, demanding a hundred bucks to turn down their boombox, insisting on their right to cross the street.

It was always something.

We knew how to handle a barking guard dog behind a chain link fence – half a bagel smeared with sticky peanut butter would buy you at least 10 minutes of silence.

But when it was a human disruptor, we called on Popeye and Buddy in their black raincoats. And sensible shoes.

They moved quick for old guys – striding right up in tandem, crowding the guy chest to chest, smothering him to where you couldn't even see what was going down. And that fast, the asshole was silenced. Usually to slink off into the night. Sometimes slumped on the pavement.

It didn't always feel right. But on a movie like this it's, "Don't ask, don't tell."

5

Woody Allen was shooting *Manhattan* while we were shooting *The Warriors*.

The two movies have something in common – both offer highly stylized versions of life in New York City. Magical Realism. When I first read *The Warriors* screenplay, I didn't know what to make of it. I figured it all depended on how it was directed.

Back then, I was a huge of fan of hyper-realistic urban dramas. *Panic in Needle Park*, *The French Connection*, *The*

Taking of Pelham 123, Taxi Driver.

Movies that cut to the bone, that smashed you in the face with a 2 x 4. (Or a Louisville Slugger.) While *Manhattan* and *The Warriors* deftly turned reality on its ear. Because even in 1978, New York City offered up a magical moment now and again.

2 a.m. I was dragging my ass home after a long shitty day searching for the bathroom for the Punks fight when I spotted a bunch of production trucks and crew members milling around on 3rd Avenue outside the Papaya King. "Nature's Own Revitalizer." Fruit smoothies and hot dogs.

It was *Manhattan* – shooting nights.

I had a buddy working as a P.A. and I spotted him hanging with Mariel Hemingway on the back lift of a grip truck. I walked up and he introduced me, and she and I chatted for a while.

She was freaking gorgeous. I mean knock down, suck the air out of your lungs, rattle your soul, gorgeous. She had the voice of a nine-year-old, but so what? She was positively delectable, plus she was six freakin' feet tall!

I fell into a love trance sitting there on the back lift of that grip truck alongside Mariel Hemingway – her wide-open face splashed with the orange and yellow neon lights of Papaya King. A trance that I could have stayed in forever.

But then my friend got called back to the set. And I knew that my own personal moment of New York City movie magic was about to end.

The devil on my left shoulder whispered, "Ask her out, dumbshit!" The angel on my right shoulder said, "She's 16, asshole. Walk away." So I said goodnight and walked away.

6

Who knew, back in the summer of '78, in the middle of shooting *The Warriors*, that Walter Hill had recently co-written and produced another movie (this one for Fox) that was shooting at the Shepperton Studios in London?

It was some kind of sci-fi flick that took place in outer space. Walter held his cards close.

One night on set in some subway station somewhere in Brooklyn, in a lull between set-ups, Walter waved me over. We'd had a few exchanges by now – nothing to write home about – I just got the feeling that he was sizing me up, and I had to steady myself around him, keep my balance. He was 36 years old, longish dark hair, scruffy beard, carrying some extra weight. He usually wore black – t-shirts, jeans. He sometimes wore a newsboy cap – herringbone, with a front snap brim. He had a style, and it worked.

So, he called me over on the subway platform and said, "I hear you want to be a writer."

"I am a writer."

"Screenplays?"

"Yeah, I've written two."

"They any good?"

"Yeah."

Walter gave me one of those appraising looks. "If you're serious, you should move to Hollywood."

I thought about it. I was single, living in a crappy Second Avenue shotgun apartment (you know, the kind with a water closet and pull chain, no shower, bathtub in the kitchen). I thought about it for all of five seconds. "Okay, I think I will."

And I did. Let me take you out of New York for a couple pages.

Walter had given me his number, and I called him a couple days after I arrived, "Hey, it's Rob, Rob Ryder. I took your advice. I'm in Hollywood."

He snorted, "Ha! You set yourself up? You good?"

Fuck yeah I was good. I'd found myself a funky bungalow in a "colorful" Hollywood neighborhood right across Gower from Paramount Pictures. Rent was $140 a month. I'd pocketed more than 6k on *The Warriors*. "Yeah, I'm good."

"Good. I want you to see this new movie I wrote. It's not released yet. My assistant will call you back with details."

An hour later I got a call back. "There's a screening set up at Warners for next Tuesday, 3 p.m."

I showed up early Tuesday afternoon. I'd never been on a Hollywood studio lot before. First time is a thrill, I don't care who you are. The guard at the gate checked a clipboard – sure enough my name was on it. He gave me a one-sheet map with the screening room circled and directions where to park. (Even though 20th Century Fox made the movie, it was being screened at Warner Bros.)

I parked, found the big boxy stucco building, climbed an outside set of stairs and walked into the darkened screening room. It wasn't all that big, maybe 200 seats. All empty. I figured I was early. I sat down for a minute. Five minutes.

Then I got up, stepped outside into that harsh L.A. sunlight and looked around. The lot was busy, all sorts of people and golf carts heading this way and that. But no one heading for the screening room. I'd expected at least a couple dozen people. Producers, studio executives, crew members, I don't know. But no. Nada. Nobody. I finally headed back into the screening room, pupils widening in the dark, and took a seat.

"That you?" It was a voice from behind me in the projection booth.

I answered, "Uh, yeah,"

"Okay, here you go."

The theater plunged into total darkness.

And the opening credits of *Alien* filled the screen.

Now look, everybody's different when it comes to scary movies. There're the hardcore buffs, the macho toughs, the teenage girls. Then me. I would rather walk the mean streets of Bedford-Stuyvesant at 3 a.m. than watch *A Nightmare on Elm Street* in my living room with five of my best friends and the lights on. And here I was. Alone. With no way out. What would I say to Walter?

Two minutes into *Alien* and I was pouring sweat, gripping the seat, knowing I was in for two hours of brilliant, exquisite movie-making torture. And when that thing popped out of that guy's chest. Fuck me…

But I rode it out until the very end. Right through the credit scroll. I staggered out of the theater, the shadows long, winter sun setting. I made it home and called Walter.

"What'd you think?"

"Fuck," I said. "Jesus. You scared the fucking shit out of me!"

Walter laughed, then barked, "Stay in touch," and he hung up. I slowly cradled the receiver, alone in my little Hollywood bungalow, full on night now.

The sound of a police helicopter passing overhead. A barking dog. Latino voices singing a wailful ballad from three back yards over.

I walked down Melrose to Bogie's Liquor on Vine, bought a half-pint of Jim Beam, went home and drank it down until I crashed.

Welcome to Hollywood.

7

Blowing up cars in movies. First you need the street. I struck out finding one, but my immediate superior, Alex Ho, came up with it. Out in Brooklyn, 62nd Street, off New Utrecht.

Not exactly what Walter Hill was looking for. (It costs a lot of dough to get an entire block of Brooklyn residents to agree to blow up a car in the middle of the night. A lot of dough.)

But Alex, being wily, finds a street that's mostly industrial, machine shops and whatnot. With a few actual apartments as well so it looks kinda residential.

Across the street a vacant lot. Alex nails it down with the residents and business owners (this is not easy shit to pull off). He then shoots a bunch of Polaroids and brings them to Walter.

"Yeah, yeah, one side looks great, but…"

"Walter, it's the best we can do. We don't have the budget, man."

"I want it to feel closed in."

"Yeah, what can I say?" says Alex Ho.

(In my experience, the production people who are honest survive the longest. But suffer the most.)

Note – Walter is under tremendous pressure here. He's slipping behind schedule. He's growing more and more pissed at his lead actor. He's clinging to his original vision of what this movie is meant to be. Just as the suits at Paramount start asking – "What the fuck's going on in New York?"

Walter tells Alex, "All right, line the opposite side of the street with semi-tractor trailers. Close the thing in like I want it."

Who gets this plum assignment? Yours truly.

Production office – 7 a.m. John Starke hands me an address (on a slip of paper, remember those?). It's the block Alex Ho nailed down in Brooklyn. "Okay, we need to rent six tractor trailers that are gonna be parked alongside the opposite side of this street. By Wednesday."

"Tomorrow's Wednesday."

Starke gives me one of those haggard looks like – You fucking moron, do you have any idea what my job is like?

I can only shrug. He tries to wave me off, but I've got questions.

"You're talking just the trailers, right? Not the tractors too?"

Starke looks at me, realizing I'm actually semi-intelligent. Not afraid to ask stupid questions.

"Just the trailers. He wants to close in the block."

"Got it. And where am I supposed to rent these things?"

"Figure it out."

"And how am I supposed to pay for them?"

Starke reaches into a secret drawer under his desk and grabs a brand-new credit card that catches the light – silver and gold platinum stars and stripes, Paramount/Gulf & Western and Glory Hallelujah plastered all over it.

"Use this."

I take the card thinking, I can disappear to Italy for the rest of my life with this card.

But no, I go back to a shitty shared desk in the locations office where I start going through huge phone books, all five boroughs, endless yellow pages, looking for where I can rent six giant trailers to be delivered to Brooklyn by tomorrow morning.

I find a place in Queens.

I catch a ride out there (without my favorite Teamster) so no, we don't talk about how the Knicks suck again this year.

We get there, at this giant lot full of big-rig trailers in the far reaches of Queens. I suck a deep breath, grasp the credit card in my pocket and walk into the office.

"Hi, I need to have six trailers delivered to this address in Brooklyn by tomorrow morning."

The guy looks at me, "Yeah?"

I pull out the credit card, nearly blinding him. "Yeah."

And it was that easy. The magic of plastic.

Four hours later I'm out on the "blow up car" street in Brooklyn as the tractor-trailers arrive. These drivers know their shit and jam the trailers up head to toe just like we want them – turning 62nd Street into an alley.

I shoot a bunch of Polaroids, check in at the production office, find out where Walter is (in the subways of course) and show up on the set.

Walter peruses the Polaroids. "Yeah. Too clean. Graffiti them up."

"Uh, okay. Sure. No problem."

Problem.

The famous screenwriter, William Goldman (*Butch Cassidy and the Sundance Kid*) wrote a book about Hollywood – *Adventures in the Screen Trade*. The most telling quote from that book – "Nobody knows anything."

So, we've got six giant blank white trailers parked out in Brooklyn. 36 hours to get them all graffitied up like Herr Director wants. Starke sends me out to "supervise" three Scenic Artists (union shoot remember?) as they paint up the trailers.

Only it takes them all morning to get half of one trailer spray-painted. Plus, it looks weird. Nothing like the New York graffiti and tagging I was used to.

By midafternoon it's clear – at this pace, this ain't gonna get done in time. I get back to the production office and tell Starke what's goin' on. He looks at me like – sheeeeesh, I thought you were good.

He tells me to get back out there first thing in the a.m. and he'll put three more Scenic Artists on it, and it's my job to make sure it gets done, because we may be shooting there the very next night.

I drag my ass home, feeling deflated. Next morning, I catch a train early. Ever ride the subway from Manhattan to Brooklyn at 5:30 a.m.? You want the definition of bleak? That's bleak.

I reach my stop in Brooklyn. Climbing the stairs out of the dark, shielding my eyes to the morning glare. I walk west and find the street of blank trailers.

Where, swear to God, every freakin' trailer has been hit by graffiti artists and taggers, and it's looking fucking great. Every trailer marked up – front to back, bottom to top. Psychedelic colors and all sorts of crazy lettering, artwork. Bubble Style, Wild Style.

And, and, some of the artwork's already been ruined by taggers – just like it's done in the subways. So it all looks street real. As street real as Walter or any nit-picking movie fan could possibly want. I wanna burst into tears, or better yet, Jay-Z:

"Now I'm in New York!

Concrete jungle where dreams are made of.

Let's hear it for New York, New York, New York!"

(In 1978, when *The Warriors* was shooting, Jay Z was 8 years old, hustling to get by in Bed-Stuy.)

8

On the first movie I worked on I had a run-in with the hyper-excitable Joe Pesci. You remember him from *Lethal Weapon* – "Okay, okay, okay okay!" And playing a lawyer in *My Cousin Vinny* – "Now I'm askin', would you give a fuck what kind of pants the son of a bitch who shot you was wearing?!"

Joe Pesci taught me a valuable lesson. If you're working production, never ever fuck with the actors. Even if they're still nobodies. 'Cause you never know.

It was out in the Secaucus swamplands. A low-rent gangster flick with a no-name cast and skeletal crew. Joe Pesci's acting "career" was going nowhere, and his old-school Italian father was bent out of shape about it. Then Pesci landed this sizable part in an actual movie.

So, he'd brought the old paisano out to prove to him he was actually gonna make it as an actor. The two of them were sitting in our only trailer, waiting for the first shot of the day.

The 1st Assistant Director was one of those frantic types – always in a panic. (Not the best role model if you're just learning how movies get made.)

I'm helping dress the set – in this case scattering some trash with the lone member of the art department – while the Director of Photography's shouting out where he wants it. The Director pacing. When the AD rushes up to me shouting, "What the fuck are you doing? Where the fuck is Pesci?! We're ready to go here!"

So, I run over to our only trailer, yank open the door and burst inside, "Joe, you gotta get to the set!"

Pesci takes serious offense – snapping his head back and slitting his eyes in that Italian-American "You fucking with me?" gangster style you see in the movies.

Pesci's father frowns – slowly turning his head from me to his son.

Joe Pesci: "What you don't knock? You don't fuckin' knock?"

"I, uh…"

"Don't rush me. I'll be there when I get there."

I smile, "You're joking, right? Come on, move it."

Then Joe Pesci – insulted like this in front of his father, goes into one of those slow-burn tirades that could've come right out of *Goodfellas*. The kind of grilling that swells your tongue and loosens your bowels.

"Let me understand this cause, ya know maybe it's me, I'm a little fucked up maybe, but you say I'm joking how, like I'm funny? I mean funny like I'm a clown, I amuse you? I make you laugh, I'm here to fuckin' amuse you? What do you mean funny, funny how? How am I funny?!"

I squirm, waiting for it to end. Waiting to be saved the way he would save Ray Liotta 10 years later. But it never came. And Pesci was late to the set.

The director wanted to fire me, but John Starke talked him out of it. So yeah, don't fuck with the actors.

9

With the guys playing the Warriors it wasn't an issue. They were good guys. Young, hardworking – determined to give Walter Hill what he was looking for.

I'd caught a glimpse of them during prep – coming into the production office to sign paperwork, looking for the wardrobe department, meeting the ADs. I registered how they handled themselves. Quiet confidence masked any nervousness.

It can be intimidating, your first studio movie. But most of these guys were New Yorkers, and the ones who weren't – you learn the ropes fast.

Later, when I first saw them out on the boardwalk in their gang attire, they really came to life. Swan, Ajax, Snow, and the rest. Looking hard in their leather vests – eyes steely, arms muscled up. They were bonding. They were a gang.

And not a star among them.

Except maybe for Thomas Waites (Fox) who had just played the lead in an indie prison movie, *On the Yard*. His character, Chilly, was "top con" on the yard, a title that gave him absolute power.

Maybe the experience went to his head because Waites started pissing people off from day one.

Fox was a critical character in the screenplay – the brains of the outfit who ends up with the girl. But several weeks in, Walter Hill had had enough.

Just that fast, Fox got thrown under a subway train, the script got rewritten, and that was the last we'd see of Thomas Waites (he didn't even get to stage his own death).

Enough has been written about Waites's firing. Except to say that he's a very talented actor/director who regrets his behavior and offers it as a cautionary tale to all the young actors who approach him at these fan conventions.

10

Side bar. Waites' previous movie, *On the Yard* was based on an award-winning novel by Malcolm Braly who had done years of hard time in Folsom and San Quentin.

I met Braly a couple summers earlier at a party at an old farmhouse in the Catskills populated by some very colorful hippies and ex-cons and slinky ladies with snake tattoos running up their legs.

I'd heard of Braly and made sure to read *On the Yard* before meeting him. Great read. He was unimposing – portly, full of good cheer. Not the hardened ex-con I'd expected. I chatted him up about his book, then about my own writing. He asked to see something, and I gave him a short story I'd stashed in the car. He called me a week later.

"So, what'd you think?" I asked.

He answered with a shiv. "At least we know you're not a genius."

11

Maybe this memory is the product of an overripe imagination, but I swear to God, sometime, somewhere before they shot the Lizzie's clubhouse scene, I caught a glimpse of the Lizzies in their original outfits. I kinda remember it being on a subway platform, and they were wearing these gauzy, tie-dye, see-through blouses. See-through as in see straight through to their breasts because they were all braless.

At the risk of offending, I'm gonna say this – these young ladies were a vision of street-tough, see-through loveliness. I remember being somewhat shocked at what they were wearing, and trying to imagine how they were gonna bounce through all that rough and tumble stunt work in the clubhouse melee without veering into *Debbie Does Dallas* territory. But when the movie came out, all those beautiful bosoms were covered up by overshirts and jackets. Bummer.

Dee Dee Benrey was the Lizzie who locked the Warriors in the clubhouse, then squeezed off a couple of wild shots as they broke down the door and ran. She missed twice. I saw her at a recent East Bay Comicon. She's doing well – living in New York, a full-fledged vegan, yoga instructor. Dee Dee's a gentle soul – and smart as a whip. (She went to Bronx Science High School.) But when I asked her about the cover-up, she hemmed and hawed a bit and I never got a straight answer.

So, I got in touch with Bobbie Mannix – the brilliant costume designer who deserves a lot of credit for *The Warriors'* unique look and feel. Bobbie's 79 now – living the good life on a ranch just outside of L.A. She's immensely proud of her work on *The Warriors* and looks forward to showing up at a few upcoming fan conventions. Bobbie said that originally the Lizzies' tops were even more risqué – with painted nipples and such – but the girls were uncomfortable with it, so they started covering up, and that's the look Walter decided to go with.

Another unsatisfactory answer. Someone put the kibosh on the boobies, and we deserve the truth. Was it Paramount's decision? The producers'? Or Walter's? I'm realizing that I'm gonna have a bunch of questions to have answered before I put this book to bed, so I'll add it to the list.

Stay tuned.

12

I was gonna save this story for later, but it still leaves a bitter taste in my mouth so screw the chronology, I'm getting it out of my system.

It was months into the shooting schedule. I'd bounced from Location Scout to Baseball Fury to Punk. We're in this giant sound stage in Queens, shooting the infamous bathroom brawl.

I'd caught some shit for moving from production to actually being in the movie. A certain amount of resentment – understandable given the circumstances. But *The Warriors* had bigger problems – running over-schedule, over-budget. And suddenly there was a Paramount exec hanging out on the set, keeping an eye on things. Remember that HBO series *Entourage*? And the character, Ari? – the smarmy agent? Dead ringer.

I'm walking across the giant sound stage to the set, which from the outside is just a bunch of cheap plywood walls, framed up with 1 x 4s. There's lights and cables all over the place. And just outside the set there's a cluster of production people sorting through the day's schedule, figuring out how they're gonna actually get through the first day on a new set. Among them Walter Hill, a couple of assistants, a production guy and this guy from Paramount – sitting in director's chairs, off to the side.

I walk past, seeing how Walter's busy with the script supervisor. But this "Suit" takes notice. "So, who do we have here, Baseball Fury or is it Princeton Fairy?"

Walter's eyes look up. Craig Baxley, the stunt coordinator, looks over. I'm on the spot. All my defensive mechanisms leaping into activation mode. I'd been heckled before. But this, coming from a Paramount hotshot, is feeling especially tricky.

"Hey, Princeton Fairy, I'm asking you a question."

I remind myself, dude, you've faced far worse than this.

On the floor of the Palestra in Philly – playing Villanova – me, the prickly sophomore – 6 foot 5 inches, 215 pounds of quick-twitch defense and sharp knees and elbows.

The Palestra was medieval, Gothic – I swear there were freaking gargoyles in the rafters. And the fans were rabid – screaming from the baselines, the sidelines – right there on the floor, right in our faces – eight thousand more looming down from the steep upper seats. Gargoyles. Screaming for blood.

As an athlete, how do you handle it? You go stone cold. Walt Frazier of the Knicks showed us the way. Do not engage. Be cool. Stay above the fray. "Clyde" was the king of the thermostat – just turned it down to stone cold. And we followed his lead. Those fans simply did not exist.

It worked back then. But now? I'm not so sure. The Suit keeps needling me, "Yeah, okay, so now the Princeton Fairy's suddenly a Punk. Where you gonna end up next, the Crisco Disco?"

I say nothing. But this asshole's getting under my skin, and he knows it. Deep down I know, hey, California Frat-Boy-Studio-Suit, you can fuck with me all you want. You can wave that Princeton Fairy shit in my face all day long. But here's something you will never know about me.

My parents were born in Brooklyn.

And my grandparents were immigrants, both sides, and they all started out poor. I mean count every fucking nickel poor. My parents never got the chance to go to college. But they knew how to work. And then me, in one generation, after slogging my way through a New Jersey public high school, I'm graduating from Princeton.

So when you call me Princeton Fairy, it makes me think about my Mom and Dad and their sacrifice, and you're burning a fucking hole right through me with this shit. But you're holding all the cards, aren't you? And you know it. And if I push back, my job's at risk.

(We've all been here. Or else you were born with a silver spoon up your ass.)

So here I am, in the hot seat, and with no other recourse, it's time to crank up the ice machine. The ultimate power of the underdog.

I'd have to do this twice more in my so-called movie career – once with Tommy Lee Jones, and once again with Shaquille O'Neal.

But for right now, it's me and Frat-Boy. And that fast, he no longer exists for me. I ghost him without even leaving. Wow, that was simple.

So, we spend days in that cavernous sound stage in Queens. Working our way through the bathroom fight. Beat by beat, shot by shot, day after day. Nailing down one of the coolest movie fight sequences ever.

While Frat-boy keeps trying to get a rise out of me. Usually within earshot of Walter who just sits there in his director's chair, looking like some bemused Buddha. Walter seemed to like it when there was negative energy flying around – as long as it didn't fuck up the shooting schedule. It juiced the vibration, and that juiced the action. But for me, Frat-boy has been iced. I've stopped acknowledging his very existence. It's kind of trippy – there's a weird vibration that it can generate – to be in close proximity with someone whose existence you refuse to acknowledge. Ever.

And eventually he just runs out of steam.

It isn't a victory. It's a stalemate. And ultimately a really stupid fucking waste of energy. I wished I'd had a river I could skate away on. But I needed the paycheck.

13

Week after week, in the bowels of the New York City subways. Hot, humid, the air stale, rank with the smell of urine. The grinding, screeching of trains.

Working locations, I was lucky enough to pop in and out, but for most of the cast and crew, it was life in a hellhole.

I head down into the subway to show Walter the Polaroids of the graffitied trailers. He's standing at the top of a dimly lit stairwell. He gives the Polaroids a quick glance and says, "Yeah, okay."

Then he looks me up and down and says, "So I heard you played college basketball."

"Yeah."

"So how tough are you?"

"Uh, I don't know…"

Wrong answer. If someone asks you how tough you are you say, "Tough enough." Or better yet, "Tougher than you."

Walter smirks. So I add, "I led the Ivy League in fouls." That brings a wry smile.

Then he motions down the stairs. "I need someone to play a cop who gets kicked down these stairs."

I look down – the stairs are steep – concrete and steel treads, and they go on forever.

Walter continues, "Ajax is gonna come sprinting up, a cop chasing him. He reaches the top and spins and kicks the cop in the chest and the cop falls back down the stairs."

I look back down the steel and concrete stairs. Imagining getting kicked in the chest and falling backwards, head first, thinking there's a really good chance of sustaining a serious injury here – as in cracking my skull open and spilling my brains from here to Union Station.

Walter's waiting, "Well?"

"No way," I say.

"Pussy," he answers.

14

You see, there's stunt work, then there's real stunt work.

Getting hit in the ribs with a baseball bat, getting slammed into a wall, that's stunt work.

Getting set on fire or jumping off a twenty-story building into an airbag the size of a postage stamp, that's real stunt work.

Falling backwards down a set of steel stairs – yeah, I'd call that real stunt work. Because it requires technique. Technique I didn't have and wasn't about to learn the hard way.

Walter didn't hold it against me.

I have a friend, David Williams, who I used to hoop with at the Hollywood Y. Dave was a real stuntman. He doubled Djimon Hounsou in a movie about a slave ship called *Amistad* (directed by Steven Spielberg).

There was a scene when the ship was out at sea, and the captain orders a bunch of slaves pushed overboard. They were chained together, tied to a giant bag full of rocks. And when the rocks went overboard, the black stuntmen followed, one by one, all chained together, hitting the water, and going deep. Deep where all sorts of shit could go wrong.

Real stunt work. But David Williams did it and pulled it off.

He laughed when he recalled the gag – "That was hairy, man. We shot it down in Long Beach Harbor. Debbie Allen was the second unit director. I came out of it with a busted eardrum, hypothermia and a skin rash that lasted for weeks. And you know about that thing called genetic memory? Well, that shit is real. Some nights, driving home from the set, we cried."

Did you pick up on that controversy about Disney making the Little Mermaid black and all these folks getting all bent out of joint about it? Like, what the fuck, between pandemics, floods, wildfires, wars, and boiling oceans, people are gonna complain about a black mermaid?

I saw David post about it on Facebook – "White folk all pissed off about how no way there can ever be a black mermaid. 400 years ago, y'all were throwing us off slave ships into the ocean. You don't think we were keepin' busy down there?"

There's black humor. Then there's real black humor.

15

Blowing up cars. Blowing up anything.

Men and explosives. Oh, boy. And when they're doing it for the movies? This shit can get seriously dangerous. And the most dangerous thing? It's almost always executed by men who not only like blowing things up, but don't get to do it often enough.

SFX Explosive Specialists, working for directors who want it bigger, louder, crazier.

Bad combo. I've been there twice.

So, let's break it down. There's a special word for the biggest fear of any SFX guy –

Antisapointment.

Imagine, you're the explosives specialist and you've just pulled off a perfectly timed explosion, big flash and bang, everybody safe and sound, and the director turns to you and says, "That's it? Really?! That's fucking it?!"

Imagine that. Now you decide how big the next charge is gonna be.

The year before Swan blew up the car in *The Warriors*, I got paid 200 bucks cash for a single day's work for a "Hey, let's blow up a car!" scene on a movie called *The Next Man* (Sean Connery).

It was one of those last-minute phone call jobs – jolts you out of sleep at 2:30 a.m. It's John Starke – the production manager who had hired me for my first movie job and later put me on *The Warriors*.

And he says, almost cheerily, "Hello, Robert. I need you today. 7 a.m. up on Fifth Avenue and 91st[th] Street. Crowd control in front of the Carnegie Hill Mansion. I'll give you 200 bucks cash."

"I'll be there."

"Where?" Starke asks, because he knows how 2:30 a.m. phone calls can wisp away like Stevie Nicks on a foggy night.

"Fifth Avenue and 91st Street."

"What time?"

"7 a.m."

"Don't fall asleep until you set your alarm."

"Yeah, yeah. John, I got it." (Never let them doubt your competency.) "So, what are we doin'?" I ask.

"We're blowing up a limousine surrounded by a bunch of pissed-off Arabs in front of an embassy."

"Uh, okay."

"Set your alarm."

And I do. But you know what? I'm gonna save that story for later. Let's get back to our movie.

When Walter Hill blew up the car in *The Warriors*, it was a simpler matter – Swan throws a Molotov cocktail at a car. It blows up. The Orphans all run away.

I got out to Brooklyn in the early afternoon – helping out on the car explosion street. Assuring everyone that we're good to go – no stray cars we'll have to move. Checking in with the owner of the machine shop. Admiring the graffitied-up trailers. Reassuring the Italian-American family halfway up the block.

Working it, as the day heads towards night. And then the crew trucks start rolling in like Patton's tanks. All business. Teamsters doing their thing.

Alex Ho (my old locations boss) walks up. "Why are you here?"

"I wanna see it."

"Okay, look, so that family, up the block there…"

"The DiMarcos," I say.

"Yeah, well, they're sorta freaking out, but they're so far up the block they're totally safe. I mean they can sit out on their fucking stoop and watch. So why don't you go hang out with them and watch from there."

I'd hoped to be closer, but yeah, "Sure."

So now it's 10 p.m. and full on dark.

The street is crawling with crew members, pulling cable, setting lights… everybody going every which way, Walter watching from his director's chair.

Then the guys who wet the streets down show up rolling out serious fire hose, hooking up to the closest hydrant and spraying water every which way to get that glistening wet street look that's working so well.

By now the vibration's growing intense, freaky almost – that electric buzz that takes over when something's gonna get blown up. Camera and sound are absolutely present – feeding off the adrenaline that's coursing through. The actors all hyped up – while the stunt coordinator, Craig Baxley, and Walter Hill walk the actors through the action sequence.

I'm halfway up the block, sweet-talking that very sweet, old-school Italian family. The old old Grandpa DiMarco, his middle-aged daughter, her kids, a cousin, a friend from next door. Sitting out on their front stoop which I've been reassured again and again is absolutely safe from this upcoming explosion.

So, the scene is set, the cameras roll, the SFX guy shouts, "Fire in the hole!"

Walter Hill grunts, "Action," to his 1st AD who immediately screams, "Action!" through a bullhorn.

The Molotov cocktail is lit and tossed, tumbling end over end, finally landing on…This shitty 10-year-old Pontiac or whatever the fuck it is out on this forlorn street in Brooklyn and blowing it up as if some Al-freaking-Qaeda super-bomb just hit it from outer space.

What I'm trying to say is it was a big explosion. It was too big.

Flash-blinding, blast-deafening, big. We all yell and spin away, covering up as I swear there's shrapnel whizzing right past us.

Then silence.

I look back to see the actors, the Warriors and Mercy, running out of the shot just like they were directed to. Then shouts of, "Cut! Cut!" Smoke clearing.

I turn to see Grandpa DiMarco literally shaking, false teeth chattering, the kids wide-eyed and whimpering, while their mother starts tearing into me, pissed as hell, shouting, how could you!? And we trusted you! And…

Alex Ho comes running up, "Hey, you're all good, right?"

"Yeah. Yeah." I see him looking up at the two-story apartment building.

"What?" I ask.

"Don't look up," he says quietly. Of course I look up, though I can still barely see or hear at this point.

A big piece of sheet metal from the blown up car is on the roof right over us, a good bit of it hanging out there in plain sight.

I turn back to Alex, "That came off the car."

Meanwhile the mom is berating not only me but now Alex, and Grandpa's about to go into catatonic shock, and the kids are moaning, terrorized.

"That came off the fucking car," I quietly repeat.

"Sshh, yeah, no shit. Just get these people the fuck to bed."

I'm still shell-shocked – and now images start lurching through my brain of me tucking Grandpa DiMarco into bed – dentures in a glass on the night table. (There's a reason why movie unions try to put a limit on the hours people work.)

I suddenly remember I'm still talking to Alex. I shake my head clear, look into his eyes and subtly jerk my head up to the roof of the apartment building.

"And what about that?"

"Forget about it. Never happened. We'll get someone out here in the morning when it's all calmed down, and they'll take care of it."

"Okay, all right. So what about all these trailers with all the graffiti and shit?"

Alex Ho, Location Manager Extraordinaire, stares at me. "Would you fucking go home and go to bed?"

"Sure." And I'm outta there.

16

"But what I really want to do is direct." Careful what you wish for. Directing a movie is about the most complicated, nerve-wracking, character-testing, gut-splitting, vomit-spewing, bleeding-ulcer inducing job anywhere ever.

What's that? Yeah, okay, I suppose General George Patton pulling off the invasion of Sicily in WW2 – 150,000 troops, 3,000 ships and 4,000 aircraft against a whole shitload of blood-thirsty Nazis is right up there.

I get it.

So: Directing is the second most difficult job in the universe. (Only Patton didn't have to make it look good.) Plus, many don't realize – the director only begins production after winning the even greater battle of getting the movie green-lit.

Months, years, of endless meetings, arguments, crushing last-minute rejections, actors falling out, inane script notes from the studio. More meetings. More script notes. Screaming matches. More rewrites. Fights over the budget.

Not to mention having to cast all the actors. Actors come with – agents, managers, lawyers – all of them convinced they know what's best for their client, and they're fucking committed to go to the mat for them. (Unless it's like too much hassle.)

Nonetheless, every green-lit director shows up that first day of preproduction ready to rock and roll (the freshest wounds masked with grip tape and a tight smile.) "Green-light adrenaline" works wonders.

Just like General Patton, a director has to visualize the outcome before even getting started. You've gotta see the forest, the whole damn thing. Only then can you get down in the trees, the weeds, the details necessary to make it all happen. Desperately clinging to that vision of the movie you're eventually gonna bring to the big screen.

First day of prep, you've got people coming at you from every angle – every one of them needing a critical question answered immediately. Camera, sound, locations, props, wardrobe, makeup, hair, and on and on. Not to mention the actors (needy fuckers, every one of them).

I think it was Sidney Pollack (*Tootsie*) who repeated that directing is like being pecked to death by ducks. Though in his case, it was getting pecked to death by Dustin Hoffman.

So, here's an example. A movie takes place over a long weekend. The make-up artist needs to know if you want your lead actor's whiskers to stay consistent or go from clean-shaven to three-day stubble. Director says, "We're shooting out of sequence."

Make-up Artist says, "I know. That's why I…"

"Can you pull that off?"

"Yes. With enough time, yes."

To a director, time is gold. Every minute of every hour is precious. To wait on an actor stuck in make-up is to die by a thousand cuts.

"We'll go with two-day stubble – all the way through." Executive decision. Left unspoken: "And if some movie nerd notices, fuck 'em." (Kinda like the Molotov cocktail in *The Warriors* that keeps appearing and disappearing.)

And that's just one of literally thousands of decisions to be made before you even start shooting.

Different directors have different styles. Alfred Hitchcock said by the first day of shooting he considered the job mostly done. He was that meticulous, that story-boarded ahead of things. It was easier for him – most of the scenes in his movies were shot on sound stages where there's total control of the elements (if not the actors).

Most directors learn to stick with their plan but be open to surprises. If your lead actress suddenly comes up with a whole new take on her character, and you see that yeah, it actually can work, you go with it.

If a talky scene on a front stoop is feeling static, you might decide to shoot your actors walking and talking down the sidewalk (sending locations, camera, sound, and just about everybody but the bagel boy scrambling to adjust.)

Or if your lead actor pisses you off one too many times, you throw him under a subway train, rewrite the script, and make Michael Beck the star of *The Warriors*.

Shit happens. Directing may not be war, but it ain't for sissies.

No wonder some directors become dictatorial. "Everybody just get the fuck out of my face and let me make my movie!" (If they have the power). For the other 95%, each day is a struggle.

Some directors choose not to fight at all. Garry Marshall directed *Pretty Woman*, *The Princess Diaries* and many more. He had a unique style. "I don't fight, I beg. I beg everybody. I beg the actors, I beg the crew, I beg the caterer. Can't we just do it this way? – it's gonna be terrific! I promise!"

17

Years after *The Warriors*, living out in Hollywood, I got the chance to work production under several directors – as a sports coordinator, choreographer, second unit director.

White Men Can't Jump was my first. Ron Shelton (*Bull Durham*) directed. We hooped together at the Hollywood Y. He knew I could play, and that I'd done production work, so he brought me on to help manage the basketball.

Shelton was tough, but fair. He listened. He worked closely with actors to achieve the nuance he was after. (Remember in *Bull Durham* when Kevin Costner paints Susan Sarandon's toenails?) And he had a unique way of pulling everyone together when things started unraveling.

Because on a movie, things do unravel. Always.

It might be because of five straight days in the hot sun with the Santa Anas blowing. Or a key location falling through. An actor feels he's not getting enough attention and starts whining. The other actors start whining in return. Then the crew's like, fuck these whiny fucking actors, and they get sloppy.

It can be one thing. Or another thing. But it's always some thing.

And the director's got to make things right.

I witnessed Shelton address this more than once (though once a movie is usually enough). He'd walk onto the set and catch everyone's attention in a loud voice. "Listen up. I'm getting really pissed off, and I think you know why! I can yell, you know! I can be a real fucking asshole! Is that what you want? Lemme know, here and now, you want me to go there? – do you want me to yell? – or do you want us to pull our shit together so we can get this movie made?!"

The cast and crew would grumble-mumble – "We're with you, Ron. We're good. We gotcha, coach."

Shelton would grin. The tension would break. And we'd be back on track.

18

I did the basketball scenes for both *Father of the Bride* movies. Director Charles Shyer. Producer Nancy Meyers. They were married and known as the Shmyers. They were extremely civilized. They had a clear vision of the movie they were making.

Charles was smart, personable, somewhat distracted. I remember him calling everybody on the crew Bubby. To the greensman: "So, Bubby, maybe those shrubs along the driveway are a little sparse…"

"Yeah, sure, you got it, Charles. Give us 30 minutes."

The Shmyers attracted all-star casts and had the luxury of long shooting schedules. Compared to my previous experiences, it felt almost leisurely – like I'd imagined old Hollywood to be.

Every day, when we began, every single detail had been accounted for – allowing Steve Martin to step out of makeup, stroll to the set (as only he could) where cast and crew would begin moving smoothly through the day's work, hardly breaking a sweat.

The Shmyers did it their way. And made some damn good movies.

While some other directors I worked under just didn't belong there. The Whoopi Goldberg comedy *Eddie* – Whoopi coaches the New York Knicks.

The director was in way over his head.

We shot for four months in Charlotte, North Carolina with Whoopi, Frank Langella, Dennis Farina, Richard Jenkins. Quality actors.

Plus, a rotating cast of real-life NBA players – Mark Jackson, Rick Fox, Doc Rivers, Kurt Rambis, Dennis Rodman… Not superstars, but real deal NBA players. Hey, we even had cameos by Rudy Giuliani, Ed Koch, Donald Trump and Fabio!

Throw in a screenplay credited to seven (count 'em, seven) different writers and what could go wrong?

Uh, how about a director who was wound so tight, who was so intent not to fuck things up, that he forgot he was directing a comedy?

Don't believe me? Check out Rotten Tomatoes. Here's one capsule review: "*Eddie* is a good example of the utter bankruptcy of creativity and originality that is Hollywood. This film has all the energy of a rotting corpse."

And then there was William "Billy" Friedkin. Friedkin had directed two of the most powerful movies ever made – *The Exorcist* and *The French Connection*. Brilliant fucking movies, both of them.

But here he was directing a basketball dramedy, *Blue Chips* with Nick Nolte as a college coach and Shaquille O'Neal as a star recruit.

It was a freaking nightmare for all of us in production. Billy had this way of at first seducing you, and then by some trick, knocking you off balance, and then keeping you in a state of absolute abject terror for the duration of the schedule.

(I'm getting PTSD just remembering.)

Thank God I wasn't there when Friedkin directed *The Exorcist*.

There were whispers back in Hollywood when *The Exorcist* was still shooting, that some really weird shit was going down on the set.

For one, imagine all the stress on 13-year-old Linda Blair – the grueling, crazed scenes she had to shoot in that bed, the screaming, the insanity, the vomit…

As JB Smoove would say, "That had to be some weird shit right there, psychologically speaking." Billy Friedkin and Linda Blair in that bedroom, day after day – wow!

But there was another whisper that wouldn't go away about Friedkin directing a priest. Friedkin had cast a real

Catholic priest in a bit part, but when his big moment came, this priest was suddenly a nervous wreck – just not delivering the performance Friedkin was looking for.

Imagine how it went down –

Exterior. Night. Winter cold. Shooting in a dark stone stairwell in Georgetown, and this real priest trying to make like an actor. They shoot take after take, Friedkin's frustration mounting. "No! No! That's not enough!"

Friedkin pulls the priest off into the shadows. "Do you trust me, Father?"

"I trust you, Billy."

"Good. Because I'm gonna help you find a different state of mind." And with that he slaps this priest, full hand, straight across his face. Not some fake movie slap, but a real, loosen your teeth and flush your bowels slap that'll sting for days.

The priest is stunned, reeling, eyes streaming hot tears. Cheek burning. Right where Friedkin wants him.

"Now let's go do this scene."

And they do.

So, yeah, directors.

(There may be another Billy Friedkin story forthcoming, but only if it's an ebb tide, the moon's waning gibbous and there's some bourbon left in the cabinet.)

Oh, shit, Walter Hill. I almost forgot him.

Walter was laconic. Above the fray. Whether you were an actor, a cameraman, a grip, a location scout, whatever – in Walter's view, you were hired because you were qualified. And it wasn't his job to tell you how to do your job. So, first thing every night on *The Warriors* as we were getting started, he'd have the ADs let everyone know what he wanted. And we'd get the job done.

19

Nobody knows anything.

Locations – we're in our usual mad scramble. We got through Coney, but there are still dozens more locations to be found, scenes to be shot. Alex Ho puts me on finding the bathroom for the fight with the Punks.

It's gotta be big, it's gotta have stalls with doors, it's gotta have sinks and mirrors, and it's gotta look like a shitty subway bathroom.

So, I hit the subways. All over Manhattan, then heading out to Brooklyn, up to the Bronx. Hitting every subway bathroom I can find. Half of them are locked shut. The other half stinking hellholes (it was 1978).

Somehow, some way, I find a few that might work. I shoot a series of Polaroids (no cell phones, remember) and head back to the set to offer Walter some choices. "Nah, too small." "Not enough stalls." "No way." Again and again.

This goes on for three days. I give up on the subways and started searching through institutions – bus terminals, the Central Park Zoo, the Met, whatever I can think of. It's freaking nerve-wracking.

But suddenly, I find it. In an aging public high school – midtown, west side. The perfect bathroom. It's big, it's got stalls, it's got sinks and mirrors. It's fucking perfect.

I shoot a series of Polaroids, panning from left to right.

Can't wait to show Walter. But where are they shooting? I find a phone booth and check in with the production office. They're in an abandoned subway station, where else?

I find my way to the set – bright lights, cables, cameras, crew, actors, all jammed together on the platform. I wait on the fringes until there's a lull in the action (do not fuck with a director when he's in the thick of it.)

I walk up to Walter, fanning the Polaroids out like a straight flush. "I got it. Check this out."

Walter peruses the pics. "I don't think so. No." Then he turns away to the script supervisor without a word of explanation. What the fuck?

As I walk off, Alex Ho grabs my arm. "Don't worry about it. Walter's been in a big fight with Paramount. He wants the bathroom built. They don't want to pay for it."

"You're kidding."

"Nope. He won. We just rented a sound stage at Astoria. Look at it this way – you helped him by not finding it."

"How long have you known this?"

"Look, you don't know until you know for sure. That's how it goes."

20

This book began with a series of posts in some of *The Warriors'* groups on Facebook. I immediately started getting cool, thoughtful feedback.

So, I want to thank all you early readers. Your engagement kept me going, slogging through this swamp of memory. I wrote and posted. You wanted more. So, I posted more. And more. And here we are.

Here's a comment that popped up from Sean Wheeldon in London –

"I heard Paramount was notorious for being tight with the budget, I think Walter Hill did amazing with *The Warriors* with the budget he had. Imagine if he had more money to spend."

Uh, maybe. But sometimes movies work best when everyone has to scrap for it, come up with cheaper, niftier ways to tell the story, to create cool effects, atmosphere.

The way *The Warriors'* director of photography, Andy Laszlo, chose to wet down the nighttime streets. Piece of cake – a fire hydrant, a wrench, and a hose. He created a great glistening look for peanuts.

Remember *Animal House*? It was made for 3 million bucks (and maybe three ounces of coke). Two years later, that same creative team turned around and made *The Blues Brothers* for 27 million (and coke, what coke?).

Animal House worldwide gross –141 million dollars. *The Blue Brothers* – 57 million. Plus, in my book, *Animal House* was the better movie. So yeah, more money, better movie? Not necessarily.

21

There's violence then there's movie violence.

The Warriors was pretty tame on the Richter Blood Splatter Scale. The action sequences were highly choreographed. Stylized.

Cyrus was the only character who got shot. The Lizzies tried their best but were the gang who couldn't shoot straight. Luther caught a knife in his arm at the end. Fox got thrown under a train. Cleon got smothered up by the Riffs (but we never even saw what happened). The Baseball Furies and Punks got beat up pretty bad. And that's about it.

Just the way Walter Hill wanted it. Like a comic book.

Nonetheless, there were violent incidents related to the release of *The Warriors*. Shit happens when you jam a bunch of testosterone-pumping young males together and jack up the volume.

Ever been to a Raiders game?

But the media hyped the public outrage, the politicians and the Guardian Angels joined the protests, and *The Warriors* died an untimely death after a promising opening weekend.

It was weird. Unfortunate.

You want a really violent gang movie? Check out Sam Peckinpah's brilliant *The Wild Bunch*. (Walter Hill was a protégé of Peckinpah's and wrote the screenplay for *The Getaway*.)

22

Locations. It's been another long-ass day, now turned night, and I'm still not done. I climb the stairs from the subway at 59th and Lex and decide to walk across to the production office at Columbus Circle.

Crossing Park Avenue, Madison, then Fifth, where 59th becomes Central Park South. Hoity toity territory, even in 1978 – all glittery and clean, leafy trees, classy buildings. Like how New York City should feel no matter what neighborhood you're in.

I'm wondering how Walter's gonna handle the big conclave scene where Cyrus gets shot and all hell breaks loose. This has been my biggest success on the movie so far – finding the location for this meeting of all the gangs. It's supposed to be in the Bronx, but when I got the assignment, I immediately remembered a spot in Manhattan's Riverside Park called Dinosaur Playground. Everyone saw immediately that it was perfect. Even Walter.

But it's gonna be a hairy production challenge – a thousand extras – all young men – dressed in crazy gang outfits. Out there night after night. Here's how the script description reads after Cyrus gets shot, the cops arrive, and a thousand gang-members panic and run:

"The police separating gang members. Pull away several from a huge melee…"

And that's it. A huge melee. Okay, so how much of that does Walter want to happen on screen? And how real is it gonna feel? Lots of ways this can go.

Ever been in a riot?

Suddenly, mid-stride on Central Park South, I'm jolted to a stop by a memory so real, so vivid, it's a punch to the gut. It's me at this exact spot, 11 years earlier. Where 6th Avenue dead-ends into CPS.

The night I experienced real mob violence.

It's the summer of 1967.

A couple of New Jersey high school friends and I make our way into Central Park for a concert – The Blues Project and John Lee Hooker. We are young, barely 16. And feeling cooler than cool.

The concert begins at sunset, ends hours later in the pitch black and is freaking amazing. But now it's over and here we are, three high school mooks from Jersey trying to decide which way is west.

It's probably 11, 11:30 at night. Through the dark, we hear a big commotion. A bunch of the crowd breaks towards it and we follow. Past the zoo, spilling out of the park onto Fifth Avenue to find a couple hundred protesters blocking traffic, causing a big mess. Carrying signs, chanting and shouting – right under Governor Nelson Rockefeller's hoity-toity New York City apartment.

Between Vietnam and all the shit at home, things are not right in America. And these people are gathered to let Rockefeller know it.

(This was one year before Martin Luther King Jr. One year before Bobby Kennedy.)

So that fast, the couple hundred original protesters swell to a couple thousand as the concert crowd brings a shitload of new energy to the scene.

Then here come the cops. A line of squad cars, lights flashing, no sirens yet, crawling down Fifth Avenue, pushing the crowd south towards 59th Street and the Plaza Hotel.

Instead of resisting, the crowd decides, fuck it, so we'll march down Fifth Avenue. And they do – we do – my high school buddies and me – shoulder to shoulder –instant members of the Marxist/Maoist New Jersey high school contingent of the Baader-Meinhof Gang.

We don't have a fucking clue. But here we are.

The crowd reaches 59th Street (Central Park South) where there's a line of cop cars protecting the Plaza. So the leaders in front veer off to the right, heading west on CPS. We all follow, leaving the cops behind. 300 yards later, the leaders hang a sharp left down Sixth Avenue. We all follow.

The energy's changing – growing electric – the cops suddenly making everything more intense, our eluding them fueling our fire. And theirs. The pace picks up, moving en masse straight down Sixth Ave. We cross 58th Street, 57th… A cacophony of shouts, screams, chants, epithets. Darker, more belligerent with each block.

And suddenly the distinct sound of breaking glass. Storefront glass. High-end, untouchable storefront glass. Huge plate glass windows being shattered left and right by protesters.

Then sure enough, a deluge of sirens and flashing lights. The cops have blocked our advance down Sixth Avenue. And that fast, they're out of their vans and attacking the front line of protesters with nightsticks.

An immediate jolt of panic and chaos sweeps through us.

I hear weird, sharp cracks zinging through the mayhem - nightsticks cracking against skulls. The surging crowd whirling in confusion.

Real violence is electric. It triggers some deep genetic response. That first jolt takes away your breath, paralyses you. While your brain races through every freaking possibility this moment holds. And reduces every possible reaction to the three FFFs – fight, flight, or fornicate.

One of the protesters from the front line comes staggering back up the avenue, hands on his head, blood streaming down his face and shirt.

Then another – his bloodied face stricken with disbelief.

The third one's a girl, running with a couple girlfriends supporting her – blood spewing from her scalp and the bridge of her nose, the girls waving off help, desperate to just get away.

Sheer pandemonium. Screaming, sirens, glass shattering. Nightsticks cracking against skulls.

My friends and I exchange a wild look and suddenly we're sprinting back up Sixth Avenue, and I mean flat out, run for your life, 40-yard dash stuff – only it's more like 400 yards – our eyes snapping left and right as squad cars – lights and sirens – come tearing in from the cross streets.

We keep hauling ass, hit Central Park South, sprint straight across, and launch ourselves over that old stone wall into the park. It's a long steep tumble down a dirt slope into some bushes. We crawl together in the dark – silent, shocked, adrenalin pumping, gasping for breath.

So yeah, shooting the conclave scene is gonna be hairy.

23

I snap out of the memory. It's almost midnight, and I need to get to bed. But first I check into the production office where the coordinator says, "Walter wants to see you."

Oh, shit, what's this about? I catch a ride to the set. They're on the Upper West Side – W. 100th St. The company has taken over an entire city block – shooting the early sequence of the Warriors catching their first sight of the Baseball Furies.

Working locations, I'd only caught glimpses of the Furies. Pinstriped Yankees uniforms, long black wigs topped by black leather baseball hats. And those grease-painted faces split down the middle by garish colors – black and yellow, black and red, then blue, then green, then purple – faces split in half. Some with black circles around one eye.

Creepy. Deranged.

They'd been working two nights and there'd been rumblings from the set – the footage looked weird, and some of the stuntmen couldn't run for shit. So, they'd brought in some track guys from the New York Road Runners and painted them up for some running scenes – but now those guys couldn't fight…

I don't know what else. Just rumors that shit wasn't going right. Then a stuntman got hurt and there was some seriously bad mojo on the set. Rumors.

I arrive and it's dark and there's a tense vibration in the air. Trucks lining the block, cables running every which way. Some cameras set up in the street. Those old school Panavision 35-millimeter cameras topped by big white magazines - mounted on heavy duty wooden tripods.

There's three crew guys tapping into a fire hydrant, hosing down the street. Everybody else standing around. I catch a glimpse of the Baseball Furies – way down the block, leaning against a building, holding bats – waiting for the next set-up.

I find Walter slouched alone in his director's chair – everyone keeping their distance.

You know how some people, when they're really pissed off, they just get real quiet, but they're fucking vibrating with negative energy? That's Walter Hill this night.

I suck a deep breath, step into his force field, and say, "Hey."

He looks me up and down. "I wanna put you in my movie."

"Yeah, okay. When?"

"Tomorrow night. Go find Craig Baxley. Tell him you're the new Baseball Fury, and he'll get you set up."

I stand there a moment, registering what's going down. Walter jerks his head – you can leave now.

So I stride off and find Craig Baxley, the stunt coordinator. He's on the corner, talking to the Furies.

Baxley's young – not even 30 – and he's got that California cool about him. Dressed in a dark windbreaker, jeans. 20 dollar haircut.

He's not some caricature stunt man. He's not gruff, he's not gnarly, he doesn't chomp on cigars. He's soft-spoken, professional. Maybe six foot one, 180. Quietly solid.

You should read his book – *Driven*. It's freaking amazing what he went on to do in the movie business.

I walk up and introduce myself. Baxley pulls me across the street, and we walk down the sidewalk alongside the trucks and trailers.

"So, you talked to Walter?"

"Yeah."

"Can you fight?"

"Yeah," I lie.

Baxley pulls me into the shadows between the huge humming generator on wheels and a camera truck.

"Okay, so how do you react when I'm coming at you?"

Baxley gives me a shove backwards, so I go into a crouch and ball up my fists. He throws a quick left jab – open-hand – that stops at the end of my nose (blood would've spurted). Then he throws a looping right, faking me out, 'cause as I block it, he plants a left hook into my right kidney. But gently.

"Okay," he says. He doesn't scoff. He doesn't call me out. He doesn't judge. "Put your left foot forward more – you're too open. Let me see you jab. Now lemme see you counter. Right cross. Punch straight. From the shoulder."

So here I am, on West 100th Street at 2 a.m., shadowboxing with a Hollywood stunt coordinator. Thinking to myself – in the script don't the Baseball Furies use bats?

Baxley gets called to the set. "Okay, stay here and work on that. I'll put you on the call sheet and see you tomorrow night. Tell make-up you're the new Purple Fury."

And off he goes.

So I stand there in the shadows, Genny humming and buzzing alongside me – shadowboxing with myself.

I'm gonna be the Purple Fury. Jesus. The adrenalin's flowing. Five minutes go by. Ten.

I'm starting to feel stupid, punching air there all by myself – crew hustling past, giving me a look now and then like what the fuck are you up to?

And I begin wondering that myself, suddenly remembering that I have an early call tomorrow – some locations shit to take care of out in Brooklyn. And now Baxley's gonna put me on the call sheet for tomorrow night, and it's gonna be right there in plain sight, and how exactly are you gonna handle this one, numb nuts?

No problem. I'll do what I usually do in a tight spot. Nothing.

Just show up for work and wait until someone says something. And I almost get away with it.

24

The next morning, 7 a.m. I show up at the production office. Maybe I catch a weird glance or two but not a word about me being the replacement Baseball Fury.

Alex Ho tells me to get back out to Coney Island. "You gotta get our stuff back from this outdoor locker we're renting under the boardwalk. The owners cut our lock off and put their own on, and we've got a bunch of cable and miscellaneous shit in there and they're holding it for ransom. It's ours. We want it back. There's a truck waiting for you downstairs."

"But how do I…?"

"Figure it out."

So, driving out to Coney in a panel truck, sitting alongside a Teamster – am I figuring out how to get Paramount's shit back? No, I'm in a trance imagining what it's gonna be like to be a Baseball Fury. I'm excited, but also aware that this is gonna be some tricky shit here. Bat fights. With real bats.

Just hours from now, at 6 p.m. I gotta report to wardrobe. Then into makeup and hair. I know the Furies are wearing black wigs, so how's that gonna work? And that creepy make-up. What's that gonna feel like?

So yeah, driving out to Coney this morning, I got a lot on my mind.

The Teamster barks, "What the fuck are you thinkin' about?"

I jolt out of my trance. And smile at the absurdity of it all. "What if I told you makeup and wigs?"

"I'd think you're some kind of fruitcake."

We drive down a street that dead-ends into the elevated boardwalk. Underneath – a walk-in cinderblock locker with a heavy steel door.

Stenciled on the door – ACME RENTS – (I've changed the name to avoid waking up with a horse head in my bed.)

I climb out of the truck and walk over to the locker. Sure enough, it's got a huge Yale padlock on it. I stare at the lock –

wondering how I'm gonna look in a wig.

A couple minutes go by. The Teamster gets out of the truck and walks up behind me. "What a guy could do here is go rent some bolt cutters."

I like that – "What a guy could do here."

So back into the truck we go and we drive around until we find this old, decrepit hardware store, and there's this hulking guy behind the counter looks like Luca Brasi, and I tell him I need to rent some bolt-cutters.

"You gotta credit card?"

Oh, do I have a credit card! (Remember Jack Nicholson in *Easy Rider*? "Oh, do I have a helmet!")

I hand over the credit card – and the magic of Gulf & Western and half of Abu-freaking-Dhabi strikes again – the glare nearly blinding him.

Luca Brasi turns and pulls a giant pair of bolt-cutters down from the wall and hands them over. I ask for the credit card back. When he gets the cutters back, he says. Fine by me, I say.

We drive back down to the boardwalk. I get out and suddenly I'm kinda tense. You try walking around Coney Island in the middle of the day with a giant pair of bolt cutters and a stupid look on your face.

I reach the locker and look left and right – nobody's watching. It's New York, I shoulda remembered. Nobody gives a shit.

Except for the guys who own the locker, but they're not around.

So, I hoist these giant bolt-cutters up and open the jaws and snap that bomb-proof Yale lock like a popsicle stick.

And it's only then I notice – written with a Sharpie on the inside of the handle of the bolt-cutters – ACME RENTS.

What the fuck?

I am struck by a wave of pure paranoia. Did I just rent these bolt-cutters from the same wise guys who own this locker I just broke into?

Is Luca Brasi right now explaining to his cousin Vinnie that yeah, he just rented their biggest bolt-cutters to some jerk-off from that fucking movie?

Uh, yup.

I never moved so friggen fast – hauling cable, light stands, apple boxes – all sorts of shit out of the locker and into the truck, and I throw in the bolt-cutters and slam the rear doors and that fast we're out of there.

Whew. Driving down Stillwell Avenue, swinging onto the Belt Parkway. The Teamster laughs.

"Looks like you bought yourself some bolt-cutters."

"And just leave the credit card…"

"So he's got a Gulf & Western credit card. What's he gonna do with it?"

I think it over. I don't know, move to Italy?

25

Three hours later I show up in Riverside Park – my first night as the replacement Purple Fury.

There's a bunch of movie trucks and trailers parked down on the grass – crew hustling about in the waning light. The sun's gone down over New Jersey, just across the Hudson River. I'm in a trance as I find the wardrobe trailer and step inside. A couple of the Baseball Furies are stripping out of their street clothes, putting on their Yankees uniforms.

The wardrobe guy looks my way. I say, "I'm replacing the guy who got hurt."

He looks puzzled. Jery Hewitt shouts from the other end of the trailer, "He's replacing Steve Chambers, purple and black."

The guy nods okay, then turns to a bulletin board filled with Polaroids of each Baseball Fury – straight on, head-to-toe photos to keep things straight. Continuity. He finds the Purple Fury Polaroid and turns. "You're a lot taller than him."

I shrug. He says yeah, okay, and goes through a rack filled with Yankees jerseys and pants and finds the right size and hands them to me, then studies the Polaroid again, "This guy keeps his jersey unbuttoned. Just tuck the tails into the pants." He shows me the picture.

"Got it."

It's all a blur as I try to put it back together. Walking from wardrobe to the make-up trailer I realize that this is really happening. It's not a lark. It's not a figment. Walter Hill has shoved this fat golden goose of an opportunity my way, and now I've got to come through for him.

I climb the three folding steps up into make-up and hair, and it's the same drill - make-up guy consulting his Furies Polaroids. Then he sits me in a chair in front of a mirror surrounded by bright light bulbs.

He draws a thin black line straight down my face – from the top of my forehead, between my eyes, straight down my nose, between my nostrils, over my lips, my chin and down my neck to the grey undershirt I'm wearing under my open Yankees jersey.

I stare at myself in the mirror as he fills in the right side of my face with some kind of thick, black make-up. Greasepaint? I don't know what it is, but it feels weird and looks weirder.

Then he checks the Polaroid and paints a black circle around my left eye. Then he paints my lips black. He finishes by coloring in the left side of my face with garish purple make-up.

Then the hair guy pins a long black wig to my hair and jams a black leather baseball cap on my head and tells me to stand up.

The make-up guy says, "Looks good."

Hair guy says, "He's taller than the other guy."

Make-up guy shrugs.

I look at myself in the mirror – I am now the Purple Fury. I am here for a reason, and I am taking this very seriously. I need to get into character. I stare harder into the mirror and tell myself - I am creepy and weird and dangerous, and I am ready to kick some serious ass. I am the Purple Fury.

I step from the trailer and join the other Baseball Furies, standing around the craft service truck eating doughnuts. It's full-on night now – the park lit in pools by production lights hidden in trees. It's getting close to my bedtime, but I'm gonna be up for hours so I down a cup of crappy coffee, then another. Craig Baxley comes over, looks me up and down and says, "Okay, let's go to work."

We follow him along a concrete pathway that cuts through the grass and trees and rises gently towards an exit onto West End Avenue. Four of the Warriors are standing there in the shadows – Swan, Ajax, Snow and Cowboy. They keep to themselves, and that's fine by me. James Remar's playing Ajax, the hothead, and Remar's doing that Method Acting thing – staying in character – a perpetual sneer on his face. The guy's been putting off a dangerous, loose-cannon vibe from day one, and I've seen how people have been steering clear of him. Me included. And now Walter Hill's about to put a bat in his hands.

We all wait there, Warriors clustered together, Baseball Furies in another cluster, several yards further on. Then Walter and his 1st AD and the script supervisor and Andy Lazlo the Director of Photography walk up and look us over.

Walter doesn't give me so much as a nod.

The script supervisor consults her notes and lines up the Warriors in the right order. Then she gets us Baseball Furies lined up – right down to which hand we're carrying our bat in.

Walter and the others head back down the pathway to the big Panasonic cameras, mounted in the dark on tripods.

Baxley watches them walk away, then steps off into the shadows, "Okay, get ready to do this."

Suddenly the four Warriors drop down onto the sidewalk and bang out a fast dozen push-ups in their sleeveless vests. Pumping up their arms, getting their lungs heaving. When they jump up, they've got their game faces on. It's a drill I've seen them do again and again, and it works, biceps swelling, faces glistening now with a thin coat of sweat.

The 1st AD calls for sound to roll, then cameras, then he shouts "ACTION!" through a megaphone. And the four Warriors take off down the dark pathway.

We Furies stand there for four beats, then Baxley barks, "Action!" from behind some bushes.

And we take off, for what? – 200 yards maybe – running hard, just under a flat-out sprint. Chasing the Warriors with bats and painted faces through the thick hot black night, and I'm thinking to myself, wow, this is different.

We chase them right past the last camera then we all pull up, sucking wind. I look over to see Walter, Lazlo and Baxley having a quick consult.

Then the AD yells out, "Back to one!"

So, we head back up the walkway and reset and do it again. And again. And again. Then we get about a 20-minute break while they move the cameras to the next set-up, deeper into Riverside Park.

I'm sweating. My shirt sticking to my back, my hamstrings tightening up. And the thick make-up covering my face must be clogging up my pores because I feel sweat backing up under my skin with nowhere to go. I observe how the other Furies are acting – checking in with each other, comparing notes.

Going through some stretches. Not a bad idea, and I join them. After the earlier shit these guys went through – what with all the fuck-ups out in the streets and Walter getting all pissed off, and then the stuntman I'm replacing busting up his leg – I can see how they've really started bonding.

Jery Hewitt is at the center of it, the glue holding them together. (Yeah, it's Jery with one R.) He's the yellow-faced Fury who squares off against Ajax in one of the all-time killer scenes ever shot in any movie ever.

Jery's just one of those guys – the kind of guy who makes everyone else feel good, feel glad to be there. He's lean, rubbery almost – a wonderful athlete. And off-camera he's genuine and generous with that smile of his. He was the first to introduce himself that night. And he's keeping things loose and funny. But once he puts on his Yellow Fury character and goes all Kabuki – that shit gets scary fast.

Cameras are good to go, so we run this next section. And again. And again.

26

The next couple days and nights are a blur of adrenalin and exhaustion. I remember the stink – crammed into a trailer filled with sweaty men in various stages of undress. And the hassle – scrubbing all that greasepaint off was a huge pain.

I remember heading home in the back of a van, crosstown, the night sky brightening with the false dawn. Climbing the stairs to my apartment, crashing for a couple hours, crawling out of bed, getting dressed while gulping down coffee. Then heading out, already late for my day job as a location scout.

I remember being met at the production office with some curious stares, but everyone being too busy to really give a shit. And I wasn't about to say anything – so I was doing a little moonlighting, so what? Don't ask, don't tell.

I dragged myself through the day and headed straight for Riverside Park for my second night as a Baseball Fury. It was pretty much the same drill – run, run, and run again. But now Baxley started pulling us aside, showing us some of the bat fight choreography he'd been sketching out. Now things were getting interesting.

But I'm dead on my feet – going on three hours sleep – trying to stay focused, keep my energy up. Thinking that maybe this double-dipping isn't such a good idea after all. The Furies scenes are scheduled for at least three more nights, and it looks like I'll be squaring off against Swan for the last bat fight of the sequence. I wonder how Michael Beck's gonna feel finding out he's about to do a flat-out, full-speed bat fight – swinging 36-inch Louisville Sluggers – toe-to-toe with a "stuntman" who's never done a stunt in his life and is all jangled up on six cups of coffee, a couple white crosses and zero hours sleep.

I put these thoughts aside, trying to stay sharp enough to make it through the night. But I know I gotta talk to the Production Manager, John Starke – he's the guy who hired me, he's the guy who got me onto my first movie for Christ's sake. I owe it to him. And to Michael Beck.

As we wrap that second night, there's a new face milling about on the set – officious looking, short haircut, white shirt and tie, glasses and probably a pocket-protector (if not, I just gave him one). He's talking earnestly to the ADs, then to some of the Warriors, and I swear he's been eye-balling me on and off, but a few hours later he's gone. Out of sight, out of mind.

I sleepwalk into the production office the next morning, determined to talk to Starke about my predicament – I want to keep my day job, at the same time honoring Walter's request for me to be in his movie. If I can just hang in a few more days, the Furies scenes will be in the can, and I can swing back into my production job, and everything'll be cool.

Before I can say a word, Starke says, "I need you to spend the day in Riverside Park – make sure no one fucks with our trailers."

"But you've got security on that, right?"

Starke stares at me.

I hate that dead space after I ask a dumb question. At least I've learned not to follow it up with something even dumber. But we haven't even acknowledged that Walter's made me a Baseball Fury, that I'm on the freaking call sheet for God's sake. Wait, is this Starke's way of cutting me some slack, throwing me a bone? Spend the day on the set where we'll be shooting that night. I don't know. I'm too brain dead to figure it out, and so I just stand there with my thumb up my ass until he says, "Get outta here."

Heading back out through the bustling office, I catch some stares, then hear someone yell out, "Hey, how's it goin', Hollywood?" And some of the production staff are snickering, teasing – it's good-natured but with an edge to it. And I'm thinking, yo, the director wanted me to be in his movie, what was I gonna say, no? What would you have done? Not to mention jumping from 50 bucks a day to like 300 or so, plus residuals. And benefits. Plus I guess I'm still making the 50 a day production pay. Double-dipping. Maybe that's where the edge is coming from.

I don't have the energy for a comeback. So, I smile and shrug – my latest go-to move.

It's high-noon-hot and sticky-humid down in Riverside Park, several security guards watching over the lines of trucks and trailers pulled off onto the bare grass alongside the walkway. I spend a couple hours sitting on a bench, drinking as much water as I can get down. Then I head over to the wardrobe trailer, brush past the security guard – "I'm with production," climb inside, curl up on the floor and fall asleep.

27

The door bangs open, and I jolt awake. It's one of the wardrobe guys. He stares at me but says nothing. I shake my head clear, realizing hours have passed, so I move to the far end of the trailer, strip out of my clothes, and start putting on my Furies uniform. Some of the other Furies start showing up, Leon Delaney, Eddie Earl Hatch (looking suave as Harry Belafonte). Then Jery Hewitt pops in and gives me a big grin.

"Rob, man, you look like the wrong end of yesterday's breakfast." I can only smile and shrug. The first couple nights as I pulled on my Furies Yankees uniform it had me feeling like a million bucks. Tonight, not so much.

I step out into the glare of the setting sun. Crew members swarming every which way – unloading trucks, pulling cable, carrying rails for tracking shots, you name it. Then I spot him, Pocket-Protector, from the night before. He stares at me then heads for the mobile production office. I climb into the make-up trailer to get my face painted.

But I'm feeling uneasy. That three-hour catnap helped, but something's off. Jery plops himself down in the chair next to me and jokes with the make-up guy, "Easy on the eye shadow, okay, Mike?" (That's another thing about Jery Hewitt – he made it a point to learn everybody's name. First time. Without fail.)

"Hey, Jery…" I say.

"Yeah?"

"So there's this guy's been hanging out on set. Wears a tie. You know who I'm talking about?"

"Yeah, that's the SAG rep. He's here to make sure we're not getting' screwed. Overtime and whatever. Good guy."

I digest this. SAG rep. As in Screen Actors Guild. As in, we don't want production staff double-dipping into coveted roles reserved exclusively for our loyal union members. Fuck. Fuckity-fuck-fuck.

I fidget as Mike the make-up guy finishes up and Frank the hair guy yanks on my black wig and jams the leather cap on over it. For the last time?

I step from the trailer to find the 1st AD, David Sosna, standing there, looking mildly perturbed. Alongside him – Pocket Protector – looking grim. Sosna steps in close.

"So, Rob, we've got a problem. You've got a SAG card, right?"

"Yeah."

I'd gotten my SAG card when I was a production assistant on my first movie, back when it was easy to qualify. Thinking it could come in handy someday, though I've got the acting chops of a streetlamp. Handy like the day a stuntman gets hurt and a hot-shot Hollywood director asks you to replace him. So at least I was legit. Okay, if not legit, legal. I had a union card with my name on it.

"You got a choice here," says Sosna. "If you stay on as a Baseball Fury you can't go back to production."

My addled brain wonders, "Ever?" – but I refrain from asking my second dumb question of the day. Instead, I ask, "Does Walter know about this?"

"Walter doesn't need to know." David Sosna was an excellent 1st AD – operating under the assumption that directors do their best work when they're not being pecked to death by ducks. I was Sosna's latest duck. And a lame one at that. "Your choice," he says.

"I'm staying a Fury," I quack.

"Good for you."

Sosna walks off. Pocket-Protector glares at me and follows after him. And I realize, holy shit, I just quit my day job. But there's no looking back. No regrets. You can't go home again. Because for the last two nights, I've been right in the thick of it – shooting a movie – lights, cameras, action, all of it, and it's been thrilling. Remember, for weeks I'd been out ahead of the process, locking down locations, working days while the real action was happening nights. Now I had the chance to be on set, for hour after hour. The chance to really experience the process.

I join the other Furies at the craft service table and gulp down a cup of coffee then pour another from the stainless-steel urn. It grows dark, the big genny humming, the trailer generators grumbling in the thick air. The muffled shouts of crew members. And now the harsh white utility lights coming on here and there. I stare at the other Furies – looking from face to glistening face in the fractured light. Yellow, Blue, Red. Orange, Green, Purple. And black. Lots of thick shiny black. It's creepy. Three nights in, you think you'd get used to it. Nope. Not me at least. Even when everyone's acting normal between setups – joking around, shooting the shit. Creepy. Deranged.

No sign of the Warriors. Something's changed. Something's in the air. The stunt coordinator, Craig Baxley, comes walking up, all business, and pulls us away from the doughnuts and leads us under a big tree where he lays out the next three nights for us. No more running. It's time for the bat fights.

28

A lot's been said about the fight scenes in *The Warriors*.

A lot of it's true. A lot of it's bullshit. And a lot of it's speculative bullshit which is the best kind.

I have learned in the last few years just how wide and deep *The Warriors*' fan base is. Worldwide. True fans. Blood loyal. A not-so-secret society. A giant family. I've learned it at these fan conventions that I started getting invited to. Where entire families show up – parents, kids, grandparents, aunts, and uncles. Friends. Brothers. Sisters. Lots of them wearing *Warriors* t-shirts, replica vests. Some even showing up in Baseball Furies face paint.

The Warriors has become a rite of passage – father to son, and now, some 45 years later, to grandson. Or granddaughter. It's very cool. It's inexplicable, but if you're on the inside, you know. You feel the warm glow of it.

And you sometimes hear directly just how deeply personal *The Warriors* runs in some people. At a recent Fan-Con in Bastrop, Texas a grizzled Latino veteran, in his mid 50s maybe, told me this – "Yeah, so I was Army 20 years. Multiple tours, Afghanistan and Iraq. In Iraq I got shot twice but they patched me up. In Afghanistan, *The Warriors*, man, that movie meant everything to us. We'd come back from these fucked-up patrols and every night we screened *The Warriors* – you know, to decompress. To process all the shit that went down that day." His eyes were lost in thought. He spoke softly. "It meant a lot to us."

And I've learned about this *Warriors* family online. Clubs, blogs, groups. But the online stuff is trickier.

Because like in every family, members get into squabbles. You see, lots of them love to speculate. Who was tougher Ajax or Swan? Who would win if the Punks fought the Riffs? You know, speculative bullshit, which will occasionally piss off one of the purists who will proceed to rag on everyone to just shut the fuck up and appreciate the movie in its original form until the speculators tell him to shut the fuck up, they're just having some fun, and they all go back to where they were.

Family. They especially love to argue about the Baseball Furies' fight and was it better than the Punks' fight in the bathroom. For my money, we should all go back and take another look at the Lizzies' fight in the clubhouse. That was some wild shit that went down there, and I think the stunt work is underappreciated.

Anyway, the thing that drives people craziest is why did the Baseball Furies just square off against the Warriors one at a time while the rest of them just stood around and watched? They had the numbers. They had the bats. They could've just swarmed them.

Reading the original screenplay, the action was thinly described. It could be interpreted any which way. One draft even has the Warrior, Cochise, running alongside the others into Riverside Park where he gets beaten to death by a Baseball Fury and thrown into the Hudson River. In the final cut, Cochise (David Harris) never even gets as far as Riverside Park and instead ends up in the Lizzies' clubhouse, making out with one Lizzie, breaking a chair over the head of another and getting home to Coney Island all in one piece.

So why did the Baseball Furies choose to fight one-on-one? There are two possible answers.

One, the Baseball Furies took an oath to fight by the Marquis of Queensberry Rules. Say what? Okay, now we're getting into the weeds but hear me out. The Marquis was a real dude back in 19th century England, and he was from Queensberry, and everyone agrees that he was one of those real fuckup, alcoholic, lying, cheating, bullying, cowardly royal lineage types. But the guy loved boxing – and ended up sponsoring a set of rules that would pull the sport of boxing out of the eye-gouging sewer pit it was in and up into the proper British world of civilized sport – tut, tut, carry-on old chap, good go!

And it worked.

The Marquis of Queensberry Rules of Engagement. Standard ring size. Twelve rounds. No head butting. No eye gouging. No hitting below the belt. Like that. So now the British upper crust could spend their Saturday nights watching two men beat the shit out of each other and show up for church Sunday morning with a clean conscience.

And since then, the Marquis of Queensberry Rules have been referenced and applied to all sorts of violent conflicts our shining species has chosen to inflict on itself. Like sure, it's cool to use the latest hypersonic three-stage solid fuel, multiple-kill kinetic-energy missile, but the Marquis of Queensberry says you can't use a cluster bomb. Logical reasoning like that.

So, that's the first explanation of why the Baseball Furies fought the Warriors one-on-one while everyone else stood around and watched.

The second? – that's the way Walter wanted it.

29

The bat fights.

Ajax (James Remar) against the Yellow Baseball Fury (Jery Hewitt). I think Jery Hewitt understood the script better than most of us. The comic book aspect that Walter Hill harbored. Jery manifested the Kabuki of it all – the painted faces, the wild wigs and costumes – a highly stylized form of Japanese theater.

The rest of us stood to the side observing as Andy Laszlo positioned his cameras and Craig Baxley led the two actors through the choreography of the first fight. Walter paced, watching as they worked on the Yellow Fury's reveal. Jery Hewitt suddenly stepped forward. "Hey, how about something like this?" And he did a little flip with the bat and Walter liked it. Then James Remar added a bit of his own to counter, and then Baxley chimed in, and suddenly it was one of those moments of movie magic unfolding, element by element, right there in front of us, contributions coming together from all different angles – climaxing with Remar adlibbing the iconic line, "I'm gonna shove that bat up your ass and turn you into a popsicle."

Movie magic. Down and dirty.

Then they went through the entire sequence for camera at half speed. Then, cameras set, they shot it. And they shot it again. And again. Then they reset cameras and broke it down into even smaller pieces. And shot it again.

Six hours later, in the wee hours, all that 35-millimeter film was canned and labeled and on its way to the lab for processing, later to be screened by Walter and Laszlo, then sent over to the editors who did an assembly, added some sound and the rest is history. You can find it on YouTube – "Furies bat fight."

So, Remar and Hewitt set the paradigm for how to shoot these bat fight set pieces, and we moved through them smoothly over the next three nights. It was impressive – watching Walter at work – with that low-key style of his, sometimes grabbing a bat during rehearsals and showing the guys what he wanted. Grunting approval.

When a movie in production has found its rhythm – after all those weeks of prep – when film is finally running through the cameras, and the cast and crew are bouncing through set-up after set-up, everybody being fed exactly what they need – whether it's a different lens or a light stand, a flubbed line of dialogue or an extra pair of rib pads – the crew always one step ahead – that's a thrill to witness. And here I was witnessing it happen night after night, fight after fight.

Until Michael Beck and I squared off for the last bat fight, and we almost blew the whole thing.

30

It was our last night in Riverside Park and people were showing some wear and tear. It ain't fun getting hit by a bat – and stuntmen were going down left and right. But the Warriors were doing a good job of measuring the speed of their swings – and the Furies were getting back up and shaking it off after every take. Everybody being hyper-aware not to smash each other's fingers with all the bat-blocking – ash on ash.

But by this last night, people were worn out – cast and crew. Michael Beck had done three straight nights of running, then had three fights over the next two nights – putting in some serious, physical hours, wailing away on one Fury after another. And now here he was, facing off with me.

Beck was a superb athlete – college quarterback, well-muscled, fit, quick on his feet. Plus, he'd been classically trained in London, and that included some stage fighting, so he was good to go. Me? The mook from New Jersey? I kept telling myself, no sweat, you got this. Just remember the sequence. Don't fuck it up. Just remember the sequence.

Walter stages it so Swan and the Purple Fury are gonna mix it up under a big tree. It's a seven, maybe eight swing sequence – Michael and I have been rehearsing it off by ourselves a bit, and now we run through it at half speed for Walter and Laszlo.

It goes something like this – he swings, I block, I swing, he jumps back, I block, I swing, he ducks, my bat hits the tree – he puts me down. I'd have to see a wide-angle master shot to recount it piece by piece (plus remember, the editor's chopped these fights into many pieces, often veering away from the original sequence).

Anyway, you get the picture. It's all been highly, precisely choreographed.

The cameras are set now – Michael Beck and me facing off in the harsh white light. Walter's in his director's chair, chewing on a toothpick. Baxley's talking us through the beats in a quiet voice, "All right, you got this. You want to rehearse it once at full speed, or you ready to shoot one?"

"Let's go for it," says Michael.

I nod in agreement.

So, we find our marks in the patchy grass, and face off, bats ready, and Sosna calls the roll, Walter grunts, "Action."

And Michael Beck rushes me, swinging hard, and I counter and it's fast and violent and right in the thick of it I'm thinking, Jesus this is fucking fast, keep up, Jesus H! Ducking, swinging, blocking, blocking again, the bats cracking against each other and now I've got Swan backed up against the tree and I swing for his head and he ducks under it – my bat cracking – ash on elm, and bouncing off and me spinning away, turning to see Swan coming at me, swinging his bat into my ribs - one, two three shots – and suddenly I'm on my back in the grass and I hear Walter grunt, "Cut," and Sosna shout, "Cut, cut!" And now Michael Beck is there, leaning in on me.

"Rob, you okay?"

I'm gasping to get some air into my lungs. "Yeah," I say, but to me it sounds like a quack. "Yeah," I say again, then add, "God, that was fast! Did that seem fast to you?!"

Michael grins down at me, "Yeah, it was fast, man. That was fast."

I get to my feet, vaguely aware that my ribs are on fire. But I'm exhilarated, and so is Michael Beck. We pulled it off. We nailed it. First take. We turn to Walter Hill – Herr Director – expecting applause. Or at least a nod of approval. A grunt maybe…

"Do it again," says Walter.

Suddenly my ribs hurt. But I keep my game face on as we head back to one. Michael's looking a little worn. We both look back to Walter like, okay, we'll go again, but what do you want different? Walter offers nothing. Michael doesn't ask. And neither do I.

As we get to our starting points, Baxley strolls up to me and says, "You know, each take you do here, it's a 50-dollar stunt adjustment."

"No shit." Suddenly my ribs are feeling better.

"No shit. And that gets added onto your daily base, so when we get into overtime…You get what I'm saying here?"
"Yeah. Let's go again."

Baxley steps out of frame. Michael and I face off, not sure what's supposed to change for this second take, so we wordlessly agree – okay, same sequence, only harder and faster.

Sosna calls the roll, Walter grunts, "Action." And here we go again.

36-inch Louisville Sluggers, slashing through the night, only harder and faster. And only this time Michael Beck – when he's supposed to leap back as I swing for his ribs – instead ducks down right into my swing – my bat heading straight for his head, and I've got visions of his brains splattering all the way up to West End Avenue, and I yank my hands in, checking, jerking the bat so it just misses, just barely bombs past Michael Beck's chiseled cheekbones, missing by maybe half an inch. If that.

Michael jerks his head back up, looking stunned, stepping quickly away as I do the same. Both dropping our bats, Walter snarling, "Cut! Cut!"

Baxley runs up, "What the fuck?"

I stare at Michael. He stares back. We both mouth, "Whoa," to each other – only he and I really understanding how close he was to a night in the emergency room. Or the morgue.

"My mistake," he says. Then turning to Walter, "I ducked in when I should have jumped back."

"Well, don't do it again," says Walter.

So, we get ourselves right, and we shoot the sequence a third time, then a fourth. Fast but measured. Hard but not so hard to splinter my ribs. Then we break it into smaller pieces and shoot several more takes. And then it's over.

And for me, this movie is a wrap.

31

Only it's not.

32

I need a minute here to clear my head. I'm more than halfway through writing this thing – I've got stories coming out of worm holes in my dreams – and I'm telling myself, keep it short, stupid. Or you're gonna burn everyone out, including yourself.

But then this happens –

As I'm trying to figure out where to put that second car explosion story, the one with Sean Connery and the Arabs, suddenly I'm remembering how that stunt was the catalyst for my first screenplay, and now that memory triggers the coolest idea for a movie I've ever had.

I'll share it with you in a New Orleans minute, but first let me lay out how I got here. (And this'll give me time to write up a quick synopsis and get it registered with the Writers Guild.)

33

I moved to New York City to write a novel. So, there I was, banging away on a battered Smith-Corona Electric – the kind where you still had to wind the ribbon and throw the carriage by hand (not exactly churning my own butter, but you get my drift – pre-computers). Mired in the kitchen of that 2nd Avenue railroad flat, 300 pages in, writing in circles, helplessly lost in this cliché of my own making.

So I started hooping again to keep my fire going. I still had a basketball jones – absolutely loved the game. Still do. As a sophomore at Princeton, I was a starter on a team ranked in the top 20 in the nation. I wasn't a scorer, I was a banger – sharp elbows and knees, quick-twitch reflexes, in there for my defense – man, I just loved to fuck up more finesseful opponents. Get up in their grills, knock them off rhythm. But 1969-70 was the most miserable winter of my life – shitty weekends on the team bus, freezing our way through New England – Dartmouth to Harvard at 3 a.m. – our star player battling injuries and illness. Plus, the coach was a real asshole – and I don't do well when people yell at me – so I quit at the end of the season.

I hung around Princeton to get my degree (and stay out of Vietnam) and here I am, four years later, living in New York with a basketball jones I cannot shake, and a novel going south so fast I could feel the typewriter wince with every keystroke. So, I one day decided to call an old teammate who was playing in the NBA and asked if he knew an agent who could get me over to Europe. Two weeks later, I had an offer to play in Finland of all places – $350 a week plus an apartment. I said yes, and since it was mid-summer, I had a couple months to work on my game.

Yeah, okay, but what about this brand spanking new movie idea? I'm getting there, all right? I'm just caught in a time-warp 2nd Avenue fruit loop and there's only one way out.

Working on my game all summer. In a constant state of hot and sweaty – shorts, t-shirts, socks always damp, hanging on a line strung across the kitchen – no washer, no dryer, no air conditioning. I played down at West 4th Street in the Village. The Cage – hot asphalt surrounded by chain link, where the level of play was high but erratic and prone to frequent interruptions involving threats, fists, knives, broken bottles, and once a jar of lye. It was the real shit, true grit, and you learned to keep your head on a swivel.

One broiling afternoon I found myself on a team with a real hot-head – Dominican I think – brown skin, long curly black hair held in check by a red headband. This guy could really play – great handles, fluid release – but man, did he have a mouth on him. And he started getting under the skin of the guy trying to guard him. This big, solid black man who didn't say a word until he suddenly just picked the loudmouth up and body-slammed him down onto the asphalt, then picked him up again and slammed him into the chain link fence behind the basket and held him there and calmly said, "Shut the fuck up and play the game."

The hothead broke free – and went off on a wild screaming tirade about how he was gonna go get his gun and kill this motherfucker and the hothead grabbed his towel and bag and shit and stormed off yelling over his shoulder about how he'd be right back and somebody was gonna catch a fuckin' bullet.

We all just stood there, open-mouthed. Whoa. Looking to each other. Some of the regulars started drifting off the court. I looked to this guy Vince I knew – white guy, always wore a Panama hat, small-time pot dealer who knew the lay of the land. And when Vince moved off the sidelines and slid into the sitting area, I chose to follow his lead. Everybody did.

Everybody except for this quiet, solid black man who'd just roughed up the hothead and now had a target on him. He didn't slide away onto the sidewalk and melt into the crowd. He didn't slip out and down into the Sixth Avenue subway stairwell.

No. He sat down on the asphalt under the far basket, leaned back into the chain link fence, put his hands behind his head, crossed his ankles and waited.

We all waited.

And suddenly there he was, the Dominican hothead, striding back up the sidewalk, holding a small gym bag in his left hand, his right hand buried inside it, spotting his nemesis sitting under the basket, yelling, "I warned you, motherfucker! I fuckin' warned you!"

And the guy just sat there. Didn't move a muscle. While the rest of us scrambled for shelter behind the concrete benches and chess tables.

Then, as the hothead came bursting through the open gate, three guys jumped him – and bear-hugged him into submission, never even taking him down to the asphalt, and yanked the gym bag away. And then they had a quiet talk with him, until finally one of them shouted out to the rest of us, "Can we get this fuckin' game goin'? We got people waitin' here who's got next!"

And we slowly walked back onto the court. Including the hothead and his nemesis, and we finished the game.

I forget who won. And was there a gun in that gym bag? I never found out. That was ballin' on West 4th.

And I loved it. And after a session, as the sun was easing down, one of my great pleasures was to buy a quart of beer at a bodega and stroll into Washington Square Park and find a bench and buy a joint for a buck – they called them bones, rolled thin and tight. Then I'd sit there brown-bagging, getting high, and sometimes there'd be a drum circle and always there'd be boomboxes, and I'd watch the colorful people stroll by, smiling, laughing, singing, holding hands, and I liked that and it was good.

But it wasn't helping my game. So I moved my scene to the leafy, slightly more civilized Central Park courts – behind the Met – where the players were a real mishmash of race, nationality and talent. And among them was a rabid Knicks fan who was making a fortune in health care communications, and when I found out he was investing in a low-budget indie movie as a tax write-off, I told him I always wanted to work in the movies and he got me on as a production assistant for 70 bucks a week, and I had to call this sports agent and tell him I wasn't going to Finland to play basketball after all, and while this movie was still in prep I got hold of the screenplay – and immediately marveled at the format – how clean and sparse it was, and I said to myself, "Fuck novels, I'm writing screenplays from now on." Lean and mean, baby – no need for all that prosy description – all those goddamn words – no need to worry about which tense I'm in (past perfect progressive my ass).

And that is how my basketball jones got me started in the movie business.

Wait, why am I telling you all this? Oh, yeah, because of this brand new brilliant idea for a movie I just had.

But we're not there yet.

So. That first Joe Pesci movie got me jazzed to write a screenplay. But I had no clue what to write about. Until that first Joe Pesci movie also led to my second movie job which gave me the clue I was looking for.

34

How to blow up a limousine in the middle of a riot.

I show up – 91st and Fifth Avenue on a freezing November morning in 1976 – 7 a.m. – crowd control on *The Next Man* – and God, they need it. A quick conference with the assistant directors – these guys are really sweating this one. Consider it – controlling a couple hundred half-crazed extras from out in Sheepshead Bay or someplace who are rioting in front of an embassy. I mean, that's gonna be challenging enough – but now they're gonna blow up a limousine right in the thick of it?

They tell me they're sticking me in the middle of the mob and my job is to make sure it looks like a real riot while making sure nobody gets killed. Uh, sure.

First a quick visit to wardrobe where they put me in a leather jacket and stick a Yassir Arafat burnoose on my head. I look as much like an Arab as Peter O'Toole in *Lawrence of Arabia* (only minus the Academy Award).

I head back to the set where there's cops and barricades and cameras and cables and crew scrambling around – and right in the middle of it, there's the SFX crew rigging this giant stretch limousine with explosives.

It's a logistical nightmare as the extras grow restless, standing there hour after hour – some breaking away to raid the craft service truck, others needing to pee, or find a pay phone or grab a few hits of weed (or is it hashish?).

I stand there, watching, listening – the director arguing with the DP, the craft service guys screaming at the extras, the SFX guys yelling at the 1st assistant director to back the fuck off.

Then the 2nd AD waves his arms, shouting, grabbing all the extras' attention – "Listen, we're losing the light! We're not gonna have time to rehearse this, so when you hear 'Background action!' I want everyone to start yelling and pushing and shit, like it's a real riot goin' on, and no laughing and smiling or shit, all right? And when the explosion goes off, you all hit the deck!"

"What's takin' so long?!" an extra asks.

The AD ignores him and rushes off. "Fuck you too, pal!" the extra yells after him.

What's taking so long is it's not enough to just blow up the limo, the director wants it surrounded by three stuntmen rigged with special harnesses so that when the bomb goes off, steel cables will yank them away from the explosion like they're being blown up. Now this is hairy shit under the best of circumstances, but on a cold November day with a mob of pissed-off extras and the light fading…

The three stuntmen are working fast – making sure the cables they're wired to are running away from the limo at the right trajectory, that the explosive canisters that'll trigger the cable-yank are good to go, and that all three nitrogen jacks are synchronized to go off with the limo bomb.

One of the stuntmen is walking towards me alongside his cable that's stretched taut right through the mob. He catches my eye – "You're with us, right? Production."

So much for the Arab disguise. "Yeah," I answer.

The stuntman keeps eyeballing the cable – from the limo across to a far light post where the cable is wired to this nitrogen jack that's gonna go off and yank him backwards through the air. This stunt man is no spring chicken – I mean, he's probably in his 50s – his face all weathered from years of stress and broken bones, barroom brawls, boozy broads and I'm guessing two packs of Pall Malls a day.

"So, where you gonna land?" I ask him.

"Somewhere between here and that brick building," he says.

The 1st AD is suddenly yelling through his megaphone, "If we don't get this shot in the next three minutes, we're dead! You hear me people?! Dead!"

The stuntman checks his cable and looks back to the nitrogen jack again. "Listen, when that bomb goes off, I'm gonna come flying right through here, all right? Like right past your head, okay?"

"Uh, yeah, okay."

"So I want you to reach up and knock me out of the air. So I don't hit that curb back there."

"Okay," I say.

The stuntman strides over to take his position at the limo.

The whole scene's feeling hyper-wired by now – crew hustling everywhere, screaming instructions. Finally, the AD calls, "Roll sound!" And the mixer yells, "Speed!" And the AD yells, "Roll cameras!" And each camera operator yells, "A camera - Speed!" "B camera – Speed!" etc. Then the AD yells, "Background action!"

And all the extras start going crazy, just like they're supposed to, even crazier 'cause they've been standing around in the freezing cold all day, and they're hungry and pissed off and they gotta take a leak, and I'm right in the middle of it with this taut steel cable running past my right ear, and suddenly BOOM!!! – the limo blows up – smoke and black cork pieces and gunpowder blowing every which way, and that fast there he is – this gnarly old stuntman hurtling through the air right at me at about 9,000 miles an hour.

I hit the deck.

And the guy screams past straight overhead.

The whole scene goes dead silent – the explosion knocking the air right out of everybody. A shock to the system. I stick my head up to see smoke rolling over a couple hundred extras all sprawled out in the street. It's surreal.

And suddenly the AD is shouting through his megaphone, "Cut! Cut! Okay! That's it, that's a wrap! That's a wrap, everyone! All you extras, go to wardrobe, sign out and go home! Thank you very much! Thank you! Go home now! And don't steal anything on the way out!"

I look back through the mayhem to the brick building where the stuntman is crumpled up in a ball. He's slowly unfolding his body, feeling for damage, his face black with gunpowder and burnt cork. Rubbing his eyes.

I walk over and he looks up at me.

"What happened to you?" he asks.

"I ducked," I say.

"Smart move," he says.

35

And that got me thinking – Jeez someone oughta make a movie about stuntmen, right? I mean, what rich fucking territory, what dynamic characters (this was pre Burt Reynolds in *Hooper*).

But what would the plot be? And I get to thinking how *The Magnificent Seven* was just about the coolest freaking movie ever made – and I'm not talking Kurosawa here, though sure, *Seven Samurai* is right up there – and yeah, okay *Samurai* did come first, but I'm talking classic American Western, John Sturges directing Steve McQueen, Charles Bronson, remember? And for all you purist Kurosawa cinephiles out there, name me one samurai from Kurosawa's movie. Just one.

While me? I'm like, Yul Brynner, James Coburn, Robert Vaughn, then Eli Wallach as the bad guy Mexican… hah! No wait, stop. I'm being an idiot. I promised myself when I started this book that I wouldn't be snarky. It's a big tent, there's room for everybody.

Okay, so now I've got this idea for my first screenplay. And I call my old college roommate who's living out in Berkeley pursuing a doctorate in philosophy while being exploited as a TA, and I say, "David, listen to this idea for a movie."

"Okay," he groans.

"So, there's this old stuntman, and he's doing one last job, his last movie, on this island in the Caribbean and the island is overrun by revolutionaries who capture the whole cast and crew and hold them for ransom. You with me?"

"Yeah."

"So word of his capture gets back to this stuntman's buddy back in Hollywood, and since no one else is gonna do it, this guy rounds up a bunch of the old gang and they make a plan to go save their friend."

"On the island."

"Yeah, on the island. You know, you get those classic scenes – these old stuntmen, all achy and rusty and shit, and one by one they agree to do just one last job."

"It sounds like *Seven Samurai*," says David.

I groan. "Name one actor from *Seven S…*" but I catch myself and ask him what he thinks of the idea, and David says, I like it, and so we spend a couple hours riffing on it over the phone, while I'm thinking to myself, you know this friend of mine is one of the hardest working writers I know – I mean, he knows how to get shit done – a thesis, a paper, another paper, reviews, proposals, grading papers, while me, solo, I'm prone to wandering around in Stephen King corn mazes. So at the end of the phone call I ask him, "You wanna write it with me?"

David, says, "Sure. Christmas break."

Three weeks later, I'm flying outta JFK into Oakland – and settling into David and his wife Meryl's one-bedroom apartment in Berkeley, and for 12 straight days, David and I drink bourbon, smoke weed, and write *End of the Rope*. And when it's finished, I fly down to L.A. with three copies and I check into Howard's Weekly Apts. on Whitley just above Hollywood Boulevard and I make it down to the Writers Guild of America and get the screenplay registered and get a list of agents, and the next day I get a roll of dimes and find a pay phone and start cold-calling agents, trying to bluster my way past the secretaries and by the time I get to the Cs on the list, I get a bite, Maury Calder of the Calder Agency on Sunset Blvd. He likes the phone pitch, so I get him the script and he likes it and David flies down and we meet this literary agent in his offices and he's effusive with praise and promises. David and I walk out on cloud nine and David heads back to Berkeley and I head back to New York, and we never hear from Maury Calder again.

Never. Ever. Never.

But here I am, 46 years later, thankful we wrote that screenplay because that memory just triggered this *Warriors Redux* idea that I'm finally about to tell you about.

36

You know how there's been this droopy-assed, never-ending debate about *The Warriors* – and are they ever gonna finally do a remake, or a sequel, or a prequel, or maybe a TV series?

And you know how most of the die-hard fans are screaming no fucking way, but it keeps coming up in conversation like a turd that won't flush?

Well, I got it. The perfect concept for a *Warriors* remake without remaking *The Warriors*. It's gonna satisfy everybody's desire for more O.G. Warriors without tainting, befouling or generally fucking up the original. This idea is feeling positively bombproof.

It's only the last couple years that I started getting invited to these fan conventions happening all over the country. Chiller Theatre in New Jersey. East Bay Comicon in California... all over the place.

It's where adoring fans come to meet their favorite actors from their favorite movies and TV shows from way back when. *Star Trek*, *Happy Days*, *Animal House*... I'd heard about these gatherings but had no idea how popular they were. And fun. At my last one in Albuquerque, I sat next to Aileen Quinn who played "Annie" in *Annie*, and she was a total doll – in her early 50s now and all of 4 foot 11 – vivacious and bubbly and so generous with the fans who came to her table for an autograph and a selfie.

Anyway, the guys from *The Warriors* have been doing these things for years – Michael Beck who played Swan, David Harris, Thomas Waites... Brian Tyler who after *The Warriors* left the movie business and became a New York State Trooper. And most of the rest of them show up too, including Deborah Van Valkenburgh who played Mercy.

They've got these booking agents and they do the rounds, several a year, and they draw big crowds, and they have a blast with it. Plus, they've rekindled the friendships – it's really cool to see them together, how they get along so well, how they love ribbing each other – and inquiring about each other's health and kids. And grandkids. And how generous they are with the fans.

If you haven't been to a Fan-Con, you oughta check one out. Not only is it a stroll down memory lane, but a lot of the fans are cosplayers, showing up in all sorts of wild costumes – so you might find yourself running into Harley Quinn, or The Joker, Jabba the Hut or Beetlejuice. Anyway, the whole thing's a hoot, and good, honest fun and nostalgic as hell and the world could use more of that.

You know what else about these conventions? There's some serious cash changing hands – greenback dollars, mostly 20s but plenty of Benjamins too – between all the celebrity signings and photo ops and merchandise and shit. Cash flying every which way.

So, imagine being at one of these conventions, say in Brooklyn say, and you've got the original cast from *The Warriors* – all in their 60s and 70s now, all gathered under one roof to meet and greet and make a few bucks.

You get where I'm going with this, right?

In Hollywood, this is called a logline –

The aging cast of an iconic NYC gang movie saves the day at a Fan Convention when a dozen real-life gangsters make a grab for the cash.

37

Am I out of my freaking mind? (What else is new?) I turn this idea over and over. I like it, I like it. But it can't be too violent. In this violent, crazed world, it's gotta be played with a light touch. Less *Die Hard*, more *Rush Hour*. It's gotta be nimble and slyly subversive. Action/Comedy.

So, we've got the genre. And the genius of this is, we already have a cast that has a built-in following. This could really work! The whole thing'll take place in one location – some fictitious convention center which we can shoot anywhere. So that's gonna give us a huge amount of control and keep the budget nice and tight.

But, uh, what about Paramount? Oh yeah, fuck. You know, the studio that owns the rights?

Paramount Pictures is a black hole where projects go to die (one of mine did at least) so I'm gonna need a workaround. How about this? I won't call it, *The Warriors*, I'll call it *The Warlords*. That's the ticket. And I'll change the names – Ajax becomes Axel, Swan becomes Shane, Snow becomes Zo, Mercy becomes Meryssa. Luther becomes Lucifer. Like that. Problem solved. Really. Just read the logline again. It could be a movie about any group of old actors – and anyone could play these characters – but if it just so happens that some of the original cast of *The Warriors* are in it, then so what?

It's an homage – look at it that way.

Like Chad Stahelski just did in *John Wick 4*. Only different.

The Warlords could be a really cool movie – what with the whole convention scene, the exuberant fans, the cosplayers. Just imagine the bad guys – wearing all sorts of weird character cosplay costumes and masks.

And the movie will have comedic riffs on how old these actors are now – what with the aches and pains and hip replacements. And we'll do some nifty set pieces and a few old-fashioned brawls with fists and elbows and teeth and makeshift weapons – chairs breaking over heads, bodies flying into mirrors. Not unlike the action in *The Warriors*.

Are you getting this? *The Magnificent Seven* meets *Rush Hour*. *The Expendables* meets *Space Cowboys*. *The Dirty Dozen* meets *Grumpy Old Men*. *Seven Samurai* meets *The Seventh Seal*? I don't know, maybe I am crazy. All I know is this logline is solid –

A group of aging actors springs into action to save the day.

We'd get as many of the original Warriors as we could, of course. David Harris, Thomas Waites, Dorsey Wright. Though James Remar might be a problem – he's been working a lot – just did a cool turn in *Oppenheimer*, plus he's still got some of that "Ajax the Contrarian" in him. But the other guys, why not? Michael and Deborah? They've still got it. They all do. So, we'll put the offer out there – see how they respond.

And maybe Apache Ramos would wanna be in it – he played the Orphan's second-in-command – "We're gonna rain on you, Warriors!" Apache's a proud Nuyorican – 30 years as a social worker, right there in the Forty-Deuce, then the South Bronx. Hard-core. Apache will bring some real spice to the party.

And how about a couple of Lizzies? Dee Dee Benrey, the vegan yogi. And Wanda Velez, another proud Puerto Rican – she's a court translator in New York – we could throw in some Spanish for her, that'd be cool.

And how about Joel Weiss? He played Luther's bad-guy sidekick, Cropsey. Great guy, talks a mile a minute, great acting chops.

And Konrad Sheehan. The Punk with the roller skates. Konrad's another fascinating cat – practicing Buddhist, has a Chinese wife, does a lot of volunteer work in the prisons. We could set up a really cool roller-skate gag for him – this spry guy in his 60s, cracking the whip, taking out some bad guys.

So not only will *The Warlords* be a great popcorn movie, it'll give the fans of the O.G. Warriors the chance to get to know these actors all over again. What they're like today.

Okay, so, let's pretend that enough of the original cast agrees to be in this movie. Where's the financing gonna come from? We're talking somewhere between 1.5 and 3 million dollars, depending on how whether we're having egg salad or roast beef for lunch.

We could try to crowd-fund it. Kickstarter or some such. Have the cast sign a bunch of posters and 8 x 10s and mail them off. Plus, anyone who throws in some dough can be an extra in the movie! And attend the premiere! That way we'd be in total control, and all the cast would have points in the movie that would actually be worth something.

Does *The Warlords* have a chance in hell of getting made? Who knows? But you know what New Yorkers say about Hollywood – "Nobody knows nothin'."

38

Okay, back to our tale (and other assorted Hollywood memories that'll make you think twice about being in the movie business).

New York City, end of summer, 1978.

It's a few weeks after my last night as the Purple Fury and my ribs are still tender – too tender to hoop – but at least the green, black and yellow bruises have gone away. I'm bored, listless. It's hot. My buddy Dominic's still up in the Catskills and I've got the 2nd Avenue railroad flat to myself.

I have no idea what the future holds. None. A move to Hollywood. Then what? Write another screenplay? Find another agent? I suppose I can knock on Maury Calder's door and ask him (channeling my best Joe Pesci) "Hey, douche bag, what the fuck happened to you?"

Then I get my Paramount check in the mail for the Baseball Furies scenes – wow, it's almost three grand! Enough to move to California, find an apartment, buy a used car. But barely. Ooh, it's gonna be tight. I'm feeling out of joint as the days slide by, knowing that somewhere in the city *The Warriors* is rolling along without me. I'm missing it. The action, the camaraderie, the bullshit.

Then the phone rings – you know, the rotary kind with the holes that you gotta stick your finger in and twirl.

"Hello?"

"Hey, it's Craig."

"Huh?"

"Baxley. Craig Baxley."

"Oh, yeah. Hi."

"Walter wants you to be in the bathroom fight."

39

Punks wardrobe fitting – I'm heading over to an old six-story warehouse somewhere on the west side. It's one of those neighborhoods where there's always trucks coming and going, guys pushing racks of clothes down the sidewalk, all kinds of contraband changing hands, and real deal Popeye Doyles sitting in unmarked cars, keeping an eye out and counting the hours. I find the building and walk into an empty space with a freight elevator. Wardrobe's on the third floor. I gingerly step into the elevator, swing the gate down and hit the button. Nothing. Then a sudden jerk and I'm grinding up to 3 where it jerks to a stop.

I step off and into rack after rack of gang attire. If you're a *Warriors* fan, this is costume nirvana. Because there it is, all of it, every gang in the movie, right there in front of me.

A sallow-faced guy walks up from the back.

"Yeah?"

"Hi. Is Bobbie here?" I'm referring to Bobbie Mannix, the brilliant costumer.

"No," the guy says.

I'm not surprised – she's got a whole wing of the production office on Columbus Circle – overlooking Central Park one way, Lincoln Center the other. "Oh, okay. I'm gonna be a Punk. They told me to come here."

"Okay," says the guy. He looks me up and down and disappears into the back.

I stand there, looking over the racks and racks of gang outfits – the Turnbull ACs, the Electric Eliminators, the High-Hats… it goes on and on. And on. It's really freaking impressive, what Bobbie Mannix has been pulling off – she and her assistants running all over the city – second-hand stores, wholesalers, street vendors, buying up all sorts of stuff, carting it back, getting it organized, constructing copies until there are nine outfits for each gang. Making magic from scratch.

The guy comes back, carrying a pair of overalls and a red jersey. He holds the overalls up to me. "We'll have to let out the straps so they're not too tight in the crotch."

"Uh, is there any makeup on these guys?"

"Not in the sketches."

"What about my hair?"

The guy stares at me like, what do I look like the hair guy to you?

A long pause, then I say, "I'll ask someone else."

"You do that. And you can go now."

"Oh. You don't need my name or anything?"

"I know your name."

"Oh."

The guy heads back into the bowels, slipping between a rack of the Boyle Avenue Runners across from a rack of the Gramercy Riffs. The Van Cortland Rangers, pushing up against the Mongols.

I hang out a bit, walking among the racks. It's really cool. And sure, it's probably cooler to me now, 45 years later – now that I've developed a fan's appreciation for the look of that movie. But it was pretty cool back then too.

Bobbie's sketches –

A few weeks ago, when I talked to her on the phone, Bobbie Mannix told me there was some collector in London who was offering to buy up all her original drawings. When we hang up, I Google "Mannix wardrobe Warriors sketches" and sure enough, they come popping up.

The drawings are rough and filled with character – strong lines, splashes of color. Swan, Ajax, Cochise – wearing those classic vests. And there's Mercy, in that pink top and skirt, although this young woman isn't nearly as pretty as Deborah Van Valkenburgh. Then there's a rendition of the Yellow Baseball Fury, and this guy isn't nearly as menacing as Jery Hewitt was to be. But it's fascinating – getting a real sense of Bobbie Mannix's process – scrolling through her original sketches.

And suddenly, there it is. A Lizzie. I knew it! Remember, me ranting about the see-through blouses and boobs and all of it? Well, here it is – proof I wasn't hallucinating on that long ago night in that rank subway station. Because this sketch I'm staring at here, this sketch of this nameless Lizzie, well the top she's wearing leaves absolutely nothing to the imagination. Unless you're imagining eight more Lizzies dressed just like this one.

I pause for a moment, jumping ahead to three weeks from now, my beta-reader/girlfriend paging through the manuscript, telling me, "You do know that all this Lizzie boob stuff makes you sound like you're still in the eighth grade?"

"Yeah, so? It's harmless, right?"

"To the six women who actually read this thing?" She shrugs. "I suppose…"

"Hey! Look, all I'm doing here is asserting the right for modern grown-ass men to still conjure up a glimmer of lust now and then – take a little detour as we mince our way through this minefield of mindfulness."

She stares at me like I've finally lost my last marble and says, "It's your book."

Huzzah! Score one for the retention of female anatomy!

40

Wardrobe complete, I head up to the production office on Columbus Circle. I haven't been back since Pocket-Protector 86-ed my production job. I walk in, trying not to mince. John Starke, the UPM, sits at his desk, mired in the muck of movie-making. He looks up.

"Hi," I say. "Just wanted to say hello."

"Hi."

I wait for more. Nada. "Walter made me a Punk," I say.

"I noticed." Another long pause.

I feel like saying, hey, John, a few short weeks ago I almost brought this whole freaking movie to a screeching halt by smashing the leading man's head to smithereens with a baseball bat, so I don't get any credit for that?

But I don't say anything, and finally Starke looks up and says, "Don't fuck it up."

Well, that's something at least. "Thanks," I say, then spin and leave, ducking some catcalls on the way to the elevators.

41

Three nights later I'm up in Spanish Harlem, Patsy's Pizzeria on 1st Avenue and 113th Street. It's just a quick shot, the first time the audience will catch a glimpse of the Punks – four of us at least. Sitting at a bar, looking surly. I find the wardrobe trailer parked out on the street, step inside, then step out a minute later, looking like Li'l Abner. Nobody's said anything about hair and make-up, so I make my way into the restaurant.

I see that Craig Baxley is there, dressed as a Punk – overalls and a striped jersey. So, he's decided to actually show his face as well as choreograph the action. Cool. Baxley's already doubled (in black-face) for Roger Hill "Cyrus" getting shot at the conclave. Plus, Baxley drove the bus with the bald-headed Turnbull ACs hanging all over it. No bombastic stunt work in that – but an eerie, visceral chase scene that sticks in the memory.

Konrad Sheehan – the roller-skating Punk – is also there, sitting on a bar stool with that choir-boy face of his – looking like a 19-year-old teenager (which he was). He introduces himself and I can immediately tell he's one of those straight-shooting, no bullshit, no hidden agenda kind of guys. Lastly – Leon Delaney who'd also been a Baseball Fury. Leon was friendly, tough, stayed in his lane – a pleasure to work with.

I'd heard that originally, Walter had wanted the Punks to have more of a rockabilly, greaser look – slicked back hair, tight jeans – but I can see that he's changed his mind. Fine by me. After all that fussing in makeup and hair with the Baseball Furies, this is gonna be a breeze.

We knock out the shot in a matter of minutes. I can tell Walter's distracted, anticipating the next scene, and the one after that. I learn that the Punks won't be needed for another couple weeks at least, and I linger around, thinking, well, shit.

But it pays to linger. After I'm done with wardrobe, I'm out on the sidewalk, watching the company wrap out and suddenly Walter's there, walking past. He nods and says, "Don't be a stranger. Come by the set sometime."

And I did. The very next night. And the night after that. And after that. I'd find out where they were shooting, and I'd show up – wearing my usual outfit – t-shirt, carpenters jeans and high-top Chuck Taylors. I haven't had a haircut in months, and now I have to keep it long since I've been established as a Punk. On these nights, I'd even help out production once in a while – off the books of course – while keeping an eye out for Pocket-Protector. Crowd control – a trip to craft services – whatever was needed. But mostly I hung around at Walter's elbow.

It was a good string of days and nights. No pressure. On me at least. But the production was falling behind, and Paramount was voicing concern. You learn a lot watching a director under pressure. Walter Hill was a cool customer. I mean, he'd say shit like, "The least we can do is lie for each other." How cool is that?

We'd talk sometimes between set-ups. Sports, movies. I was a little tongue-tied at first, and looking back, I wish that one Dale Carnegie rule of conversation had been drilled into me better – ask questions. People respond. Especially if they're older. It's flattering and doesn't have to be obsequious (which is a fancy word for smarmy, only different).

I mean here I was – hanging out on a subway platform with a man who'd been the 2nd Assistant Director on *Bullit* with Steve McQueen! *Bullit* – one of the all-time classic, lean and mean action movies – tightly paced, expertly constructed. And I never asked him about it, the things he might have learned. And here I was hanging with the same man who wrote a screenplay that Sam Peckinpah directed – *The Getaway* (McQueen and Ali McGraw). And I never asked him about that either. And then he directs his first movie – *Hard Times* – starring Charles Bronson – one of my favorite tough guy actors of all freakin' time – *The Great Escape*, *The Magnificent Seven*… And did I ask him a word about it? Nope. Numb nuts.

Ask questions.

But, hey, way back then, maybe it was better that I didn't ask. Because whenever anyone recounts their years in Hollywood, it always turns into a cautionary tale - movie veterans offering up 50 different reasons to try another profession.

42

48 Hours – a cautionary tale.

I've been in Hollywood almost four years, making some headway as a screenwriter. Still living in my cheap bungalow off Gower and Melrose (in the shadow of Paramount, but better yet, kitty-corner from Lucy's El Adobe – margaritas and enchiladas verdes).

When I first arrived, I'd picked up a job at Paramount as a propmaker. Banging out sets for *Mork and Mindy*. Then during pilot season working these long ass shifts – 6 a.m. to 6 p.m. – seven days a week. Building all sorts of crazy shit. We once built an entire underwater sea laboratory for a TV pilot – *Catalina Sea Lab*. Not a straight line in the blueprints and we built it all out of plywood. That was the job when I was way high up in the rafters, rigging a fly-away hatch, and I dropped this huge 10-pound turn-buckle and the thing punched a hole right through the ceiling, and the other carpenters didn't talk to me for the rest of the day. After you put in enough weeks, you were required to join the union – Local 44 – but I told myself I didn't move to Hollywood to be a propmaker, and so I hung up my hammer.

Two months later, I got a script optioned. Then scored a writing deal with an indie. Then I somehow snagged a real-deal agent at the William Morris Agency. A fastidious Englishwoman, Judy Scott-Fox.

Her words still echo in my head after a disastrous pitch meeting, in that clipped British accent, "Now we don't want to do that again, now do we?" She set me up with one more WGA deal then pawned me off to two junior agents.

It hurt. But I had a credo back then –

Keep your head down. Keep writing. Just keep fucking writing.

Seemed like a good idea at the time.

Jason Williams was this boisterous crazy-talented white NBA player. "White Chocolate" they called him. Reflecting on his time at the University of Florida, he said, "I wish I'd spent less time studying and more time working on my jump shot."

Me looking back – "I wish I'd spent less time writing and more time hanging out in the right bars."

In Hollywood, sure it's about talent. But more importantly, it's about who you know.

Anyway, one more day in the Hollywood flats, grinding away on my IBM Selectric. The phone rings. It's Walter's assistant, Mae Woods, calling out of the blue. "Walter wants you to attend a sneak preview of his new movie. It's called *48 Hours*. It's this Friday night, down in Long Beach. Can you make it?"

"Yeah, sure. I'll be there."

"Your name will be at Will-Call. And Rob, you should know. Paramount is extremely unhappy with how it turned out."

I hang up, intrigued. Friday afternoon I jump in my Toyota Corolla and grind my way down the 101, then the 110, crawling through downtown L.A., picking up the 405 and finally arriving at one of those giant old-school Southern

California movie theaters. The parking area bigger than C-Lot at LAX. I park and head towards the box office.

To this day, Will-Call gets me all trepidatious. I mean, just because you call doesn't mean they'll answer. But sure enough, my name's on the list and suddenly I'm in this giant lobby of this giant movie theater where they're selling giant barrels of popcorn and those giant cups of soda that'll put you into diabetic shock just looking at them.

I'm early, but the lobby's starting to fill in.

I turn to the left and spot a group of grim-faced Paramount executives clustered together – blue suits and salon hair-cuts – arguing. Jabbing fingers into each other's Armani buttonholes.

Uh-oh.

I pan across to the right of the lobby. Walter Hill, looking defiant. Mae Woods. Larry Gordon, the primary producer. I see Larry say some last words to Walter then start the long walk across the lobby to the Paramount executives. Another dead man walking.

But Larry's one of those tough guy movie producers – "I'm a Jew from Mississippi. You think you're gonna fuck with me?"

I head over to Walter and Mae Woods.

"Hey."

"Hey."

And that's all we say. Standing there watching hundreds and hundreds of people stream through, heading to find seats.

It's a mixed crowd, just like the real Long Beach. Black, White, Latino, Asian. On the rough side. Skeptical about what they're in for – but hey, it's a free ticket.

I take one last look across the lobby. Larry Gordon in a heated conversation with the suits from Paramount. I nod to Walter and Mae and head inside to find a seat.

The theater is filled, packed, with I don't know, 1,200 people? With no idea of what to expect. Only that it's Nick Nolte, who everybody knows and thinks, yeah, okay cool, Nick Nolte. And Eddie Murphy, who anybody who's been paying attention knows he's been absolutely tearing it up on SNL the last two seasons.

The lights go down. The movie starts. A convict work gang along a California back road. Classic long lens shots and piercing music by James Horner carrying over opening credits.

And then there's James Remar (Ajax from *The Warriors*). One convict among a dozen, swinging a pick – a guard with a shotgun watching over them.

And then shots of a battered truck speeding, fishtailing up, Sonny Landham at the wheel. (You'll recall Sonny Landham played a cop in *The Warriors*, and a Cajun in *Southern Comfort*, and a role in my personal life called too close for comfort.)

Action sequence. Pick-up roars in. Sonny Landham starts a fake fight with James Remar. They roll into a muddy ditch, Landham slips Remar a gun and they jump up, guns blazing. Two guards die and they get away.

The action sequence is intense. There's a visceral reaction from the audience in Long Beach. Okay, Walter, so far, they're with you. You can feel the vibe in the theater.

So, the bad guys head into San Francisco where they track down another bad guy looking for their money. This is David Patrick Kelly (Luther of the clinking bottles fame in

The Warriors).

Then we slide into some of Nick Nolte's private life as a cop. Arguing with his sexy girlfriend, blah, blah, blah.

I look around the theater – the crowd is hanging in but growing restless.

"Where's Eddie Murphy?"

Then another terrific action sequence – guns blasting away at short range – sexy women screaming – men breaking through glass doors.

Wow! A good action sequence on the big screen – that's intense. The audience catches its breath.

But then there's a long sequence with Nolte back at police headquarters and a lot of movie-cop-yelling.

Down in Long Beach, this hodge-podge, blue collar redneck, black pride, Spanish speaking, date-night audience – begins to stir.

"Where the fuck is Eddie Murphy?"

Good question.

The movie is 25 minutes in when Nolte finally enters the prison to free up convict Reggie Hammond for 48 hours to help him catch the bad guys.

What? You make the audience wait 25 minutes for the star of the movie?

But it's an iconic character reveal. The convict, a very young Eddie Murphy, in his prison cell, headphones on, singing "Roxanne. You got to turn on the red light. Turn on the red light. Roxanne…!"

And that audience, down there in that gi-normous movie theater in Long Beach, California, suddenly goes electric. Goes ballistic. Goes fucking crazy as Eddie Murphy hits that falsetto: "Turn on the red light…"

And just like that, Walter has them in the palm of his hand. And he dances them through another 65 minutes of wise-cracking mayhem and that audience is freaking roaring in pure unadulterated delight, right through the end credits.

The lobby's a chaotic mess. The Paramount executives spraying each other with self-congratulatory sputum.

While Producer Larry Gordon tells them, in so many words, I told you so, you stupid fucks.

And Walter Hill is nowhere to be found.

I drive home to Hollywood, wondering what the fuck I've gotten myself into.

48 Hours grossed 76 million dollars.

Soon after, Paramount hired Walter to make the sequel.

43

We're back down in the subways.

Transitioning from nights to days can be a real shit show for cast and crew. Mentally and physically. And a movie like *The Warriors* where all the exteriors were nights, made scheduling a nightmare. Because all the other stuff was interiors and could be shot during the sunlight hours. All the subway scenes, the Lizzies' clubhouse, the bathroom. That's a lot of interiors there – where everybody can work normal hours. Or at least daytime hours.

But movies made on a tight budget have to be nimble – some locations have limited windows which can suddenly fly open and the whole production has to immediately shift gears. And sometimes interiors are shot at night just to avoid another killer transition.

Like I've said, the whole movie-making process is grueling. People get worn out.

But me? I'm in heaven.

For one, I'm on the call sheet again. On the clock. Dressed in overalls and a red jersey – no make-up, no wig – breezing along. We're shooting the approaches to the subway bathroom fight, and I'm keeping my own personal shot list.

Shot #1 - Walk up to Konrad and Baxley, lean against a tiled column, and look mean.

Shot #2 - Keep leaning against the column and keep looking mean.

Shot #3 - Follow Konrad and Baxley through the arcade and look mean some more. (And try not to close your eyes, dumb-ass.)

Maybe I was counting my money. I'd already gotten the full SAG day-rate for that quick shot in Patsy's Pizzeria. And now we're two more days into the subway fight scene, and nobody's even thrown a punch.

It's fun watching Deborah Van Valkenburgh do her scenes underground with Michael Beck. And then the stuff where they're joined by the rest of the Warriors. Not just watching her work but having to be in her actual sightline as Mercy and

Swan glance over at us.

Deborah Van Valkenburgh – all 5 foot 3 of her – probably suffered more actual physical damage than anyone else in the whole movie. When Walter had had enough of Thomas Waites, he decided to kill his character, Fox, off early by throwing him under a subway train. Mercy was in the scene with him – Fox grabbing her hand as they run away from the cops. Baxley couldn't find a stuntman who'd make a good double for Waites, so he recruited an assistant cameraman who could've been his doppelganger. But during one take, this assistant cameraman stumbled and fell, dragging Deborah down with him instead of letting go. Compound fracture of the wrist – and the reason why Mercy appeared in the rest of the movie wearing a windbreaker to cover her cast.

Deborah Van Valkenburgh later got hit by a bat above her right eye – stitches and make-up – and she never missed a beat.

She was a gamer.

She'd graduated from Pratt Institute in Brooklyn with a BFA in Painting & Drawing. She was also musical and appeared in the Broadway musical, *Hair* before being cast as Mercy in *The Warriors*.

Mercy, Mercy, Mercy.

Once she was cast, Deborah Van Valkenburgh grabbed the part, sunk her teeth into it and didn't let go. She wasn't an obvious choice, but she was the perfect choice, and she knew it – "This is my version of Mercy, and if you don't like it, blow me." (Something Deborah would never say, but Mercy would.) She lived that character straight through the shooting schedule. As essentially the lone woman, Deborah did some masterful navigating, on camera and off – in the midst of all that testosterone, so many big dangerous dudes coming and going.

She wove her way through it like a pro.

Unflappable.

She also became close friends with Marcelino Sanchez who played Rembrandt. On a day off, the two of them went to see Walter Hill's *The Driver* (with Ryan O'Neal and Isabelle Adjani). Deborah and Marcelino both loved the beautiful French actress – and when we were shooting the bathroom fight scene, they'd turn to each other and mimic that pouty shocked French look of hers. So, if you catch either one of them suddenly vamping like Isabelle Adjani, you can blame Walter Hill.

44

Astoria Studio is out in Queens – not far from where I was born in Kew Gardens General Hospital. My parents grew up in Brooklyn, but after the war my dad scored a job with the United Nations, and they ended up living in this housing development called Parkway Village. It was built to accommodate all the international UN personnel of color who'd faced discrimination in the NYC housing market. A lively, friendly neighborhood of a hundred languages and nationalities. How my folks ended up there I never learned.

Astoria Studio was built in 1920. It's where the Marx Brothers shot *Animal Crackers*. It's where Gloria Swanson shot

Manhandled. The gigantic sound stage was steeped in history and practically reeked of cigar smoke and Chanel No. 5. By the time *The Warriors* arrived in 1978, the site had been listed on the National Register of Historic Places.

I'd never been on a sound stage before. They have these gigantic sliding doors that can accommodate the biggest trucks and flats and whole sets and whatever other gigantic creation some director wants on his set. And yeah, they still have those classic red lights and bells that go off just before cameras roll. They're cavernous – ceiling way way up there, criss-crossed with catwalks and rigging and all sorts of wires and lights.

It's my first day showing up for the actual Warriors/Punks fight. I step inside, my eyes blinking, adjusting to the dim light. In the center of the space there's a big square wooden room – exposed 1 x 4s and plywood and diagonal bracing – walls maybe 10 feet tall – each side about 25 feet long. It looks small in the huge space. As I walk up to the entrance to the bathroom – I remember the scene that connects Union Station to this set in Queens.

It's the scene where Mercy says to Swan, "I can't go in there. It's the Men's Room." And Vermin suddenly appears, "Are you kiddin'?" grabs her arm and yanks her in. If you find that scene on YouTube and run that shot again, you'll see Deborah deliver one of the coolest comedic moments in the movie – her mouth flying open, limbs akimbo – as she's yanked offscreen. But don't blink, it's that fast.

Anyway, as I walk through the entrance and onto this set for the very first time, my jaw drops. It looks so freaking real – the grimy tile, the green stall doors, the funky urinals. It looks as real as the high school bathroom I'd found weeks earlier, realer even, and for a moment I wonder if the production designer had somehow gotten ahold of the Polaroids I'd shot.

No matter.

I was hard on the scenic artists earlier – for milking the trailer/graffiti job, but the folks who built this bathroom did fantastic work.

The rest of the cast begins to arrive – Deborah, Michael, Brian Tyler, David Harris, Marcelino Sanchez, Terry Michos, Tom McKitterick.

They've found their rhythm by now. Learned each other's quirks and habits, formed bonds, established methods of working through a scene beat by beat. They were good together, and I was looking forward to mixing it up with them.

45

Probably my favorite takeaway from *The Warriors* is the camaraderie of the group. The congeniality. Despite all their differences. Let me step out of the box for a minute to say this – in many ways, *The Warriors* has become more meaningful in this fractured world than ever before. Than ever intended. A shining example of how we can all just get along.

The Warriors were truly interracial. And it was also cool how all of them made sure to look after Rembrandt, who was clearly gay. Marcelino Sanchez never hid who he was – he didn't have to – the other guys accepted him like a little brother, on camera and off. They knew he wasn't a fighter, he fulfilled a different role for the gang. (But you can ask Konrad

Sheehan how it felt to be at the wrong end of the hard right Rembrandt threw.)

And consider the other characters – Cleon, Swan, Ajax, Cochise – how sure, they had their differences – but it was never about race.

Look, we live in a harsh, cruel world.

And that's where these modern-day Warriors are doing so much good – showing up at these conventions – demonstrating by example, despite all their differences, how easy it is to get along. Spreading love among this giant *Warriors* family that just continues to grow.

It's a big tent that's been created – people of so many races, nationalities, religions – gathered in spirit to celebrate this band of brothers who were just trying to find their way home. I've made friends with fans from Italy, Japan, Brazil – all over the world. People of every stripe and color. It's a kick. It's heartening.

Not long ago, a picture of the wonderful Native actor, Gene Braverock, popped up on Facebook. He was wearing a *Warriors* vest – looking over his shoulder, tough as nails. He's done a shitload of movies, and you can catch him on TV in *Dark Winds*. I tracked him down – *The Warriors* meant a lot to him growing up. As it still does for so many other Natives.

So yeah, this is a plea for understanding. Yeah, I'm talkin' to you, *Warriors* family – we can have such a positive influence. Show the world what it means to get along with each other. Make that extra effort to understand what life must be like for someone who didn't come into this world built just like you. How did that old Mary Lathrop poem put it? – before we judge or accuse –

"Take the time to walk a mile in his moccasins."

46

Or walk a mile in his Nikes.

White Men Can't Jump. It's early morning on the Venice Beach courts – socked in, waiting for the marine layer to burn off. It's only our second or third day, and cast and crew are still finding our footing, working out the dynamics. But this movie is a winner. Even this early into the shoot, we all know it, and it's one of the best feelings in the world. On day one, Wesley and Woody lit the fuse, turned this sucker into a rocket ship, and we are gleefully along for the ride.

I'm hanging with the director, Ron Shelton – going over the day's scenes – mapping out the basketball. We're within earshot of couple dozen players, shooting hoops in the chilly fog, calling out, laughing, scarfing down breakfast burritos and hot coffee. The steel rims clanging, chain nets snapping. The surf a dull roar from across the empty sand. Waiting on the sun. I finish up with Shelton and walk onto the court – exchange a few good mornings, throw up a couple jump-shots.

One of the balls is flat. I look around but can't find the prop guys, so I start walking down the Venice Beach walk towards the prop truck when I come upon Kirk, the incredibly crusty sound mixer (aren't they all?) who's rolled his sound cart as far away from the set as is humanly possible and still be working on the same movie.

Kirk has a little BMX bike that he keeps to hustle in on when he's needed. I ask if I can borrow it, and since he hasn't had the opportunity to hold something against me yet, he says yes.

I jump on the bike and sprint down the empty walk through the fog, when suddenly I hear a loud voice yell, "Hey, you! Stop!"

I keep riding. Venice is filled with lunatics. When some stranger yells for you to stop, you don't.

Suddenly I hear the whoop whoop of a police siren. I immediately get that queasy feeling in my gut and skid to a stop.

Two cops drive their black-and-white up the walk through the fog, stop and climb out. One white, the other Latino. The white guy has a hair up his butt.

"Hey, asshole, why didn't you stop?"

"I didn't know who it was."

"You didn't know who it was?"

"That's right."

"I'm a police officer."

"I didn't realize that."

"Do you realize it now?"

"Oh, yeah."

"Oh, what?"

"Yes."

"Yes what?"

"Yes, I realize that."

"No, you mean 'Yes, sir.' Right?"

"Uh…right. Yes, sir."

"Did you realize you were breaking the law?"

"I didn't realize that."

"You don't realize too good, do you? What are you some kind of dumb-ass?"

I say nothing.

"Answer me, dumb-ass."

And on and on it goes. My mouth clenching against the urge to say something really stupid that might cost me one of the coolest jobs I've ever landed. So, I stand there and take it as he systematically chips away at my dignity, at my manhood, until finally his Latino partner grunts something unintelligible and this white cop decides he's had enough and lets me go.

I walk the bike back to the sound guy and stalk back to the courts, burning with anger and resentment. And it shows. A few of the players walk up. Most of these guys I know. We hired right off the courts we played on – Venice Beach, the Hollywood Y, Poinsettia Park. Wonderful ballplayers, great guys. Men. We didn't hire gang-bangers or fuck-ups. Half of these players had college degrees, jobs. Responsible members of society.

"Rob, man, what's up?"

"I, uh…I just got hassled by a cop."

"For what?"

"For riding a stupid fucking bicycle on the walk."

"Wow, man, you look seriously pissed."

More players wander up and start peppering me with questions.

"They cuff you?"

"Uh, no…"

"They make you spread on the ground?"

"No."

"Put a foot in your back?"

"No."

By now these players are exchanging looks.

"They put a gun on you?"

"No."

And there it was, the first smirk.

"They make you go to your knees and crawl backwards towards them?"

"Uh, no…"

"Then what'd they do, man?"

"They, uh…the guy was a real asshole."

"You're sayin' he talked mean to you?"

And by now the smiles are busting out, and I realize, man, I'm cooked – pity the poor white boy. I try to save it by saying, "Yeah, he was a real meanie."

But by now these guys are laughing, and now they're doubling over laughing and slapping fives laughing while I just stand there like an idiot, half-smiling, until finally the roars subside and I say, "Fuck all uh yuhs."

And they laugh some more.

47

But guess what. We need our cops. And before allowing an anti-cop backlash to get out of hand, we've got to walk a mile in their shoes too. It ain't easy for all the good cops out there, in these crazy times, navigating that thin blue line. And with this country of ours – and the way 2024 is shaping up – that thin blue line has got to hold.

What'd they use to say back in the '60s? "If you don't like the police, next time you're in trouble, call a hippie."

Aw, man, now I'm gonna catch it from just about everybody, so guess what, how about I let Chris Rock try to bail me out here?

"I know being a cop is hard. I know that shit's dangerous. I know it is, okay? But some jobs can't have bad apples. Some jobs everybody gotta be good. Every-single-body. Like… pilots! Ya know, American Airlines can't be like - *Most of our pilots like to land. We just got a few bad apples that like to crash into mountains. Please bear with us.*"

48

A.J. Bakunas is a hard-ass, and he lets everyone know it.

We're back on the sound stage at Astoria Studio, shooting the bathroom brawl.

Craig Baxley's been beefing up the stunt team. He's already got four of us Furies playing Punks – Jery Hewitt, Leon Delaney, Eddie Earl Hatch and me. Then he's got Konrad Sheehan and himself. Then he brings his stuntman cousin, Gary Baxley, in from Hollywood, plus Tommy Huff. And then he invites A.J. Bakunas to the party.

Bakunas is over six feet tall. And he's built solid. A few months earlier he'd broken the world record for a free fall in the movie *Hooper* – 238 feet into an airbag.

A few weeks after that, another stuntman, Dar Robinson, shattered Bakunas's record. 286 feet.

So yeah, A.J. Bakunas arrives with a chip on his shoulder. He isn't an asshole exactly. He's just arrogant.

We spend the first day rehearsing how the bathroom brawl's gonna go. It's a big, complicated piece of action – 16 gangbangers beating the shit out of each other, over and over, in an enclosed space. Chains, knives, bats, mirrors… Teeth. Craig Baxley's running the rehearsal and he's good. Clear, concise. Walter and Andy Laszlo looking on intently – discussing camera angles as Baxley walks us through it.

The Punks' entrance. Then lining up in front of the stall doors. He blocks the movements, step by step. Konrad on his roller skates, yanking open that first stall door. Rembrandt spray-painting his face, then throwing that straight right hand.

And on and on. We first rehearse in slow motion, then at half speed until we know how it's supposed to go.

A.J. Bakunas goes through the motions with the rest of us. He isn't disruptive. He doesn't cause any scenes. But there's a vibration emanating off him that's making me uneasy, so I steer clear.

Sure enough, the next day as we start shooting this highly choreographed piece of violence, Bakunas can't hide a contemptuous sneer.

It finally boils over as Jery Hewitt completes the gag where he gets clocked by a left hook thrown by Vermin, and he spins and flies backwards. Jery puts his special Kabuki sauce into the mix and really sells it. Then he limps off camera to join the rest of us who've been standing to the side, watching, and he looks at us in that genuine, wide-eyed, "aw shucks" way he has.

"So what'd you guys think?"

"That's gonna look like shit," says Bakunas.

A long silence.

"What?"

"It looks like a fucking cartoon, man. The way you're playing this. All a you guys."

We're stunned – what the fuck?

But Jery's from New York. "Did you hear Walter complaining?" No response.

"So you didn't hear Walter Hill complain."

Bakunas is stumped.

Jery heads for craft service. "I need a cup of coffee. Anybody want a coffee?"

You see, Jery Hewitt understood Walter Hill's vision from day one. Bringing that extra bit of style that makes the action pop. Way ahead of the rest of us.

And way over A.J. Bakunas's head.

49

Leon Delaney died. Like me, Leon played a Fury and a Punk. It hurts when I get the news. He was a good man. It makes you reflect, as yet another one of us bites the dust.

For me, it brings out the old doom and gloom my sons are always teasing me about. Some of us, by nature, prepare for the worst, bypassing that "hope for the best" part entirely. The news of Leon Delaney's demise makes me want to trot out the meme I post every spring – "Don't forget, the clocks go forward tonight, as they do every night, pitiless and unstoppable, silent witnesses to our inevitable decay."

But then this pops up – literally as I'm writing this – posted by my Orphan friend, Apache Ramos. It's a recent quote from Bonnie Raitt – "Life gets mighty precious when there's less of it to waste."

I went out with Bonnie for a while, back in the day – a great gal, high-spirited (certainly more than I could handle) but she knows of what she speaks. Because for years, Bonnie Raitt has quietly cared for some of the great old blues singers – musicians who made their mark, then quietly slipped into obscurity, poverty, decrepit nursing homes. Bonnie's witnessed it again and again over the years, and she's done what she could to ease their pain.

So yeah, life gets mighty precious.

If there's any takeaway from this mess of words I've assembled here, it should be this – we've got to be kinder to each other. We've got to find the love in our hearts.

There are others we've lost from *The Warriors*.

Jery Hewitt. He died in 2020 of a brain hemorrhage – some chunk of flotsam or jetsam that'd been jostled loose years earlier, maybe while doing a gag on *The Big Lebowski*, or one of the 13 other Coen Brothers movies he'd worked on. He knew it was floating around inside his skull – his doctor had warned him – but he didn't let it stop him from being the husband, father, son he was born to be.

Sonny Landham died in 2017. Now there was a man who lived a colorful life. And now that he's dead, I can finally tell my story about him (to come).

Marcelino Sanchez died in 1986 – Rembrandt. The gay Warrior, beloved by his brothers in arms.

Paul Greco died in 2008. He was the leader of The Orphans – a fine actor.

A.J. Bakunas died in 1978, just days after we finished shooting the Punks/Warriors bathroom brawl. In a world record-setting free-fall in a movie called *Steel*. 315 feet, almost 30 stories, off a skyscraper in Lexington, Kentucky. He hit his airbag dead solid perfect traveling 115 miles an hour. It split wide open. He died the next day.

There are others. And there will be more. It's sad, but inevitable.

As for me – I'm planning on sticking around for a while. This damn world is too damn interesting not to see what's gonna happen next.

It's nice to see how Deborah and the Warriors are taking care of themselves as we all slide into old age. They show up at these conventions – lean, fit, and spry – raring to go.

I've learned that there's two ways of growing old. The easy/hard way. Or the hard/easy way.

The easy/hard way goes like this – you say to yourself fuck it, I've paid my dues, I'm gonna live my life my way – and so you hit the booze and hit the cheeseburgers and cheesecake – just indulge the shit out of yourself – 'cause you deserve it, goddammit. And you do. And if the price you pay is diabetes, or neuropathy, blood clots, gout, angina, osteoarthritis, erectile dysfunction, sleep apnea or any of a thousand other ailments that'll turn you into a miserable, crochety old whiner whose vision of victory in this glorious life has been reduced to a successful bowel movement, then so be it.

Then there's the hard/easy way. Because it's hard work eating all those fucking vegetables. But it makes it easier to get up off the couch without groaning.

And as long as I'm on this slippery soapbox – for all you younger folks out there – get your nasty-ass habits under control while you still can.

And then there's this – we all have to take better care of our mental health. Especially us guys. Men. We're allowed to talk about all this crazy shit we're going through.

And yeah, we should pay attention to our spiritual selves as well.

I was blessed to be able to care for my aging mother during her last years. Like most people who live long lives, my mother experienced a whole lot of challenges and a whole lot of hurt along the way. The Great Depression, a young husband gone off to war, the loss of a child (my kid brother, Mark). But my mother somehow, some way, kept her spirits up, kept her faith, kept her hope for humanity alive.

Finally, after 95 years, she was ready to die. She went out with a lot of class – loving up her kids and grandkids, thanking her caregivers. On her next to last day, I asked her, "Mom, if there's one thought you'd want to leave us with, what would it be?" (Expecting her to deliver some beautiful piece of spiritual advice.)

She thought for a moment and said, "Take care of your teeth and your feet."

So, yeah, for all you Warriors out there – take care of your teeth and your feet.

And each other.

And this fragile little blue marvel of a planet that all 8 billion of us call home.

Because it's all we got.

50

Sonny Landham was the most dangerous man I ever met.

He played a subway cop in *The Warriors* – the cop who gets taken out when Swan throws a bat at his legs. I steered clear of him on *The Warriors*. But wasn't so lucky on *Southern Comfort*.

It's 1980. I've been in Hollywood two years. I've written my third screenplay and gotten it optioned to a producing team in Toronto. For all of two thousand dollars.

My first writing deal.

But the money runs out, and I've given up my propmaker gig at Paramount, so I find a job down in some empty hangar at LAX, up on a scaffold, painting the 1 x 2 cross-braces that keep the rafters from twisting. There have to be 5,000 of these things. By the end of the day, I've hardly painted 500.

Getting paid maybe 4 bucks an hour. (Federal minimum wage was $3.10 an hour back then.)

I drive back to my Hollywood bungalow beyond depressed. But then I find this message on my machine: "Hey, it's Walter. I got some stunt work in my new movie for you if you're interested."

If I'm interested? If I'm interested??!!

Three days later, I'm flying first class to Shreveport, Louisiana, to work on *Southern Comfort*. The SAG minimum is $315 a day, plus overtime, plus stunt adjustments.

On the plane with me are three real stuntmen.

Ned Dowd, a former minor league hockey player whose sister Nancy wrote the movie *Slapshot*, based on Ned's life in the minors. (Ned Dowd had a great role in the movie – the fearsome enforcer, Ogie Ogilthorpe.)

Then there's Allan Graf who played left guard for the undefeated USC national champion football team in 1972 and went on to become a leading Hollywood stunt coordinator.

And then there's Sonny Landham. Sonny was older than us by 10 years or so. Before his legit movie career, he'd been a Baptist Minister and a porn star. After his movie career, he spent three years in prison then ran for Governor of Kentucky on an anti-Arab platform. He got married five times. He was half Cherokee, part Seminole, part Irish and all crazy.

We got drunk on the plane and listened as Sonny told story after story in that deep baritone voice of his. And that laugh... Remember *The Shadow*, "Who knows what evil lurks in the hearts of men? The Shadow knows!" That laugh. Only scarier.

We stagger off the plane, get driven to the Sheraton Shreveport and check in. What a relief to finally be in my own room. I take off my shoes and flop down on the bed. 30 minutes later the phone rings. "Hey, it's Sonny. Come up to my room – 217. I got something to show you."

Oh, fuck. I put on my shoes, climb the stairs to the second floor, walk down the hallway and knock on 217. "It's open," comes that deep voice from inside.

I swing the door open and step into the dimly lit room. The door clanks shut behind me. My eyes adjust to the light and there's Sonny Landham, standing alongside the bed.

Stark naked.

Now this man is 6 foot 5 and an easy 235. Muscled, chiseled. Straight black hair hanging down over one eye.

He's holding a 15-inch Bowie knife.

He raises the knife so the blade catches the light, and he smiles that wicked, sinister smile of his.

"Whaddaya think?"

"Uh, wow," I stammer. "Really nice."

"You wanna hold it?"

"Not right now," I answer. "In fact, I gotta go."

"No, you don't."

"Yeah, I do. I forgot something. I forgot I gotta go call my girlfriend."

And that fast I'm out the door and striding down the hallway, the sound of Sonny's deep cackling laugh echoing after me.

We have an early call the next day, and at 8 a.m. we're out in some swamp on the Texas/Louisiana border – the crew trucks parked along both shoulders of a muddy back road. Everyone realizing what a miserable fucking shoot this is gonna be.

We were told to check in with wardrobe, but I first find my way to the food truck and order a breakfast burrito and coffee. Sonny Landham saunters up and orders the same. Neither of us says a word.

RIP Sonny Landham.

51

The hardest thing for a screenwriter is to be working on a movie in another capacity, in a production job. Because you know what? – nobody wants to hear, "I'm actually a screenwriter." There's only one thing you can do in these situations – bite your tongue. Well, my tongue's got nothing left but stitch marks and scar tissue.

Don't get me wrong, I had a nice run as a screenwriter. Within two years of moving to Hollywood, I started scoring development deals. I optioned an original spec script. Then I scored an option rewrite deal on another spec – with the wonderful Englishman, John Irvin signed on to direct. Then I scored my first studio deal at 20th Century Fox. (Now known as 21st Century Fox but owned by Disney.) This was a big break for me. See, there was this crazy stuntman turned director, Hal Needham, who had just come out with *Cannonball Run* with Burt Reynolds, about a car race across America and the thing made just under a jillion dollars. So the guys at Fox got the bright idea to do their own *Cannonball Run*, but to make it a car race around the world. Of course, there was the sticky problem about what to do about all those oceans, but they counted on one of the screenwriters they were interviewing to figure it out. So, I figured it out – 86 the cars, the oceans remain – and I landed the job and delivered a solid screenplay. But the executives who hired me got fired and suddenly Fox wasn't so hot on this project (I called it *360*). These guys landed across town at Paramount and tried to get it made there, but no luck.

Speaking of Paramount, I later wrote a romantic comedy about a group of African-American twenty-somethings who go off on a river-rafting trip. *Take Me to the River*. You know, a fish-out-of-water, black-men-can't-swim kind of story. It was actually pretty good. Funny. I was playing ball with some actors at the Hollywood Y and one of those guys was dating Jasmine Guy who was starring in *A Different World* – and he got it to her, and she loved it – we actually did a table read in the conference room right there in the Y. Then Jasmine Guy gave it to Debbie Allen who was directing and producing *A Different World*, and she loved it and wanted to direct. So, a few weeks later Debbie Allen and I marched it into some executive's office at Paramount and pitched it and they loved it, and we left the script and walked out, and we never heard from them again.

Now get this – three years later, I rewrite the same screenplay, change the title to *Sink or Swim*, make sure the page count is different, find a new agent – this young hot shot who was selling spec scripts like crazy – and he's enthusiastic over the phone, so on a Thursday afternoon, I deliver the screenplay to his office, right across from the William Morris Agency in Beverly Hills, and I grab my young wife and our two-year-old son and we go off backpacking in the Sespe Wilderness above Ojai. Get back late Sunday night and the message machine is smoking hot. What the fuck? I rewind the tape and sit down and listen. It's my new hot-shot agent – "Rob, where the fuck are you?! We're getting offers!" Then, "Seriously, man, you gotta call me back! I got Disney, Warners and Paramount going crazy here!" Then another message, then another – "We're gonna lose the deal here, I don't say yes to somebody! Call me! Where the fuck are you?!" And finally, "Okay, decision made – we're goin' with Paramount. Option-rewrite, six figures."

My first reaction? – cool! My second? – uh-oh.

Should I tell this agent about Debbie Allen and my previous foray with *Take Me to the River* at Paramount? Uh, by now you're familiar with my m.o. when it comes to critical decisions – so I do what I always do. Nothing. Don't ask, don't tell.

Three days later I show up at Paramount for one of those gushing, we love it, we love you, we love your work, now here's what we want changed kind of meetings. Luckily, it's with a different pair of executives. So, I sit there, and listen, and then I go off and do this rewrite and turn it in, and never hear from them again. *Sink or Swim.*

Now get this – 30 years later – I rewrite the screenplay yet again – this time setting it at an eco-resort in Belize, playing up that black-women-don't-camp angle, and I'm hoping to get it made. *Take Me to Belize*. Please.

I had a bunch of other development deals. One with Ron Shelton at Tri-Star. Never got made.

Another with John Hughes at Warner Brothers. Never got made.

But I was a working screenwriter. Legit. Union card and everything, though this card I earned the hard way.

Even Walter Hill hired me – it was sometime after *Southern Comfort*. Walter was making movies, one after another, and he was rolling in dough. He called me in and pitched me this idea about a skip-tracer in Texas. Wanted me to co-write it with him. WGA deal – his production company was paying.

So, we hammered out the story, then Walter went off onto his next movie and told me to write the first draft and I did. Even came up with a cool title, *Dead by Morning*. But I kept veering away from the original storyline we'd hammered out, and when Walter finally read it, he pretty much shrugged. I was crushed. I couldn't convince him how worthy this screenplay was. He did give it to Powers Boothe who'd won an Emmy for his Jim Jones portrayal and had starred in *Southern Comfort*. Powers Boothe dug it, so he and I met Walter for lunch at the Formosa Cafe and plied him with sake and egg rolls, trying to convince him to make *Dead by Morning* his next movie. No luck.

Crushed again. Walter did say I could shop it elsewhere – so my agent got it to this very capable TV director who loved it and brought it into Warner Bros. where it got excellent coverage, but Warners passed and *Dead by Morning* was DOA. I got hold of the coverage – a standard three pages – genre, logline, synopsis, comments. I just dug it out of an old banker's box buried in my garage. Wiping away the spider webs and mouse turds. Here's what it said –

"*Dead by Morning* is classic Walter Hill. The writing here is top quality. It's quick, action-packed, character-driven, and polished. The story moves along with precision and economy, and the unfolding of the detective mystery is solid and clear-cut. Along the lines of *48 Hours*, it combines high action sequences with great, underhand comedy. The characters are bolstered and enriched by touching, humanistic shadings. Overall, this is a classic action/adventure script."

Jeez.

Maybe I'll bring it up with Walter – hey, man, I know you've got your next project lined up, but how about making *Dead by Morning* the one after that? Shit, you're only 79 years old, fuck, Clint Eastwood's 92 and he's still directing. So yeah.

The glamorous life of a Hollywood screenwriter.

52

In Hollywood, screenwriters are given only so many lunges at that gold ring, so many shots at turning one of these development deals into an actual movie. And after a while, the deals dry up. The agent stops returning your calls, and the newspaper starts landing in the only puddle in your driveway.

But if you're lucky, like me, you can stay in the business by returning to production work.

When Shelton invited me onto *White Men Can't Jump* to help with the basketball, that led to a whole new line of work. I was suddenly a sports specialist. After *White Men*, there came a run of other sports movies, commercials, TV shows. And I'm still at it – a great side-hustle – mostly directing voice-overs for EA Sports videogames these days. It's a cool gig – hiring a bunch of athletes, putting radio mikes on them and running them through their paces – grunting, groaning, talking trash – NBA Street, NFL Madden, FIFA Soccer and lots more. The last one I just finished was UFC 5. These jobs are fun, they're fast, and they help pay the bills as I continue to bang my head against that screenwriter's wailing wall of insanity, still looking for a different result.

I mentioned working on *Eddie* – Whoopi coaches the New York Knicks. Kurt Rambis and I handled the basketball, down in Charlotte Coliseum, North Carolina. Rambis managed all the NBA stuff, working the phones, wrangling the players and coaches. He had a fat rolodex and a likable manner, and he spent most of the movie hanging in the coaches' office, making calls and shooting the shit. While I was out on the hardwood, dodging hand grenades. So yeah, *Eddie* ended up with 7 credited screenwriters – I watched them come and go, from the start of prep right through shooting – sometimes solo, usually in pairs – overpaid and clueless how to find their way out of this swamp of a screenplay they'd inherited. I would read each draft as the new pages magically appeared, printed on the latest color of the week – because once the production ball is rolling, any changes to the script have to be easily located. On *Eddie*, new pages kept piling up until the colors were flying around like confetti at a gay pride parade that took the wrong turn.

I struggled through each new draft, finding flaws, coming up with solutions – it was the screenwriter in me – but who could I tell, Kurt Rambis? So, I kept my head down and slogged through the production, biting my tongue to the bitter end.

Whoopi and I got along okay, though, man, she is one tough cookie. At one point between set-ups in the near empty arena, I was sitting in a courtside seat, my head buried in a shot list. Whoopi came over and plopped down in the seat next to me. She was beat. She knew *Eddie* was a dog and her vibration was really low.

I grunted hello and kept my head down. She nudged me with an elbow and said, "What the fuck are we doing here?"

I looked up into her eyes. "I'm here for the paycheck."

She stared at me, brain turning, "While I… so the real question is, what the fuck am I doing here? Oh, thanks a fucking lot."

"I didn't say it."

"You didn't have to."

So yeah, *Eddie* hurt, but at least it was a pain that affected all of us, a collective misery that permeated every nook and cranny.

The movie that hurt the most – *Father of the Bride*.

Because several years before *Father of the Bride*, I was hired by John Hughes's company at Warner Bothers to write a comedy for Steve Martin. That's right, the same Steve Martin that I'm right now teaching how to spin a basketball on his finger.

John Hughes was a unique, extremely gifted writer/director. *The Breakfast Club, Ferris Bueller's Day Off, Planes, Trains and Automobiles.* He made bright, smart, funny, well-constructed movies that we all loved. He wanted to do another movie with Steve Martin, and he came up with this one-line idea – Steve Martin is a single, nerdy guy living in New York City when he suddenly gets swept up in a romance with a beautiful foreign model who it turns out is only in it for the green card.

That was it. That's all they gave me to work with. I never even met John Hughes – to me he was like the Wizard of Oz – this mythical being – when actually he was back home in the Chicago suburbs, living a normal family life. But the money was real, and I got to work.

The first thing I did was give this character a job – made him a low-level curator at the Metropolitan Museum in the Arms and Armaments Department. Perfect. Hughes's people liked it – it gave Steve Martin all sorts of possible sight gags – like the time when no one's looking, and he tries on this knight's helmet and the thing gets stuck and he has to get back to his office without getting caught. Like that.

I plowed through the screenplay and was about to turn it in to Warner Bros. when another movie was suddenly announced by Disney – *Green Card* – with Gerard Depardieu and Andie MacDowell.

And another one bites the dust.

And here I am, a few years later – on the set of *Father of the Bride* – hanging out at this beautiful house and garden out in San Marino – teaching Steve Martin and the effervescent

Kimberly Williams how to play basketball.

It was wonderful – Steve was gracious and had good hands (probably due to all the magic tricks he'd worked up). He and Kimberly were bonding like the perfect father/daughter, him taking her under his wing. Because she was a true ingenue – a first-timer – and here she was, 19-years-old, starring in a big Hollywood movie with one of the most recognizable stars anywhere ever. When they first met Steve said to her, "Welcome to Hollywood. Now find yourself a good therapist."

Martin Short and Eugene Levy would stop by, just to hang out and shoot the shit, and when the three of them got to riffing, the whole crew would start drifting over, waves of laughter rolling over the backyard until one of the ADs had to get everyone back to work.

I always kept a basketball under my arm, and I'd grab Steve and Kimberly whenever I could, and we'd go back to the little one-hoop court in the back driveway, and we'd work on some stuff.

And I could tell he appreciated me – didn't just take me for some jock. How many times did I almost grab him and say, "You know, a few years ago, John Hughes hired me to write a movie for you."

But then what? I could imagine him just staring at me. Because I was the basketball wrangler. And it would've have been too big a shift for his already overloaded brain to digest – at least that's what I told myself. It would've been unfair to him. I mean, what's he gonna say, "Oh, that's nice?" So I held my tongue.

The night we finally shot the scene – father and daughter playing one-on-one in the driveway – was the best night of my life.

Charles Shyer, God bless him, showed up sick as a dog. I'm talking the worst possible flu and fever – he should've been in the hospital on multiple IVs – but he wanted to grit it out. It was his movie, and he was gonna be there. It was a chilly night. We were getting things together. The cinematographer, John Lindley, setting lights so we could bounce through multiple set-ups without resetting again and again.

Charles Shyer shuffled out of the house, wearing an oversized parka and beanie, bent over, shivering. He climbed up into his director's chair and called me over. He could barely talk. I am not exaggerating here. And he said to me, "It's all yours, Bubby."

And for the next eight hours we just rocked and rolled that scene, knocking out shot after shot, set-up after set-up, checking them off the list, ad-libbing a bunch of stuff, trying this and that. Laughing, shouting. Me, actually in the driver's seat, barking out "Action!" and "Cut!" just like you see in the movies. All of us having a blast, and Steve was happy, and Kimberly was happy, and the crew was happy, and even Charles sick-as-a-dog Shyer was happy, and I was happy too.

53

"I thought this book was about *The Warriors*."

So did I. We're closing in on the end. Here's a bunch of random *Warriors* stuff I couldn't find a place to work in –

Dorsey Wright played "Cleon" the leader of the Warriors until he got killed at the conclave. Michael Beck played "Swan," the guy who took over. Back in 1978, when we shot this thing, Dorsey Wright was all of 20-years-old while Michael Beck was 28.

Craig Baxley planned on having Luther's Cadillac hearse make a jump onto the beach at the end. They'd even built a ramp for it, but the production ran out of time and money.

Everyone gives the Lizzies a hard time for being so inept at firing their guns. But an early draft of the screenplay had Vermin getting shot and killed by a Lizzie. Terry Michos saved himself by creating such an endearing character that Walter decided to keep him around through the end.

Speaking of Lizzies, I never did find out how the Lizzies's see-through, titillation cover-up actually went down. Let's just call it a collective decision – and a wise one for all concerned. Modesty can be a virtue.

Lin-Manuel Miranda is turning *The Warriors* into a Broadway musical. Miranda's a real talent, the guy who did *Hamilton*, and a New Yorker through and through. He said he's going back to Sol Yurick's novel to create his stage musical version. I, for one, wish him well. Seriously, this could be really really cool – big, loud, in your face, poignant. But his is a tricky task, because *The Warriors*' movie fan base runs broad and deep, while the novel's, not so much. Try threading that storyline needle. But if anyone can pull it off, it's this guy.

When the writers' and actors' strikes started shutting things down, I decided to put my energy into a musical of my own – *Hoop de Ville*. It's actually a live arena show – a juiced-up *Harlem Globetrotters* – but with a big emphasis on the dance teams, music, cheerleaders and mascots. I've got drumlines facing off, mascots going toe-to-toe, dancers strutting, streetballers bringing it, cheerleaders doing that "call-and-response" thing with the audience. There's so much talent out there – guys like Grayson "The Professor" Boucher who's a friend and has promised to help with the hoops, and then there's Beyonce's choreographer JaQuel Knight, who tested ideas for us at an early workshop. Talent like that.

Now all I need is some big name to help me get *Hoop de Ville* launched. Someone like uh, uh, Lin-Manuel Miranda! Yeah, that's the ticket! Like he said in a recent *Rolling Stone* interview – "Ask the thing you want to ask while your hero is in front of you! Don't be a dick, don't be obnoxious. But also know that you may never get that opportunity again." So yeah, Lin-Manuel Miranda, my hero, how about it? You know how to reach me.

Uh, actually you don't. So, it's – purplefury78@gmail.com.

And that email's good for anyone else who wants to touch base, weigh in, or generally shoot the shit. Just don't go busting my chops by pretending you're Lin-Manuel Miranda.

If you're looking to order a signed copy of the book, or maybe some photographs, or check out where and when the Warriors and the rest of us will be making personal appearances, please go to www.purplefury.net.

The Baseball Furies may have played by the Marquis of Queensberry's Rules, but Ajax sure didn't. You can go back and catch him nailing Harry Madsen (the Blue and White Fury) from behind while Harry was just standing there like a dumb-ass. (I mean you wouldn't at least have your head on a swivel in the middle of a bat fight?)

Throughout the movie, the rest of the Warriors never once talk about losing Cleon. Or Fox. Maybe that's part of the appeal of this cult classic – just skip all the sentimental parts. Man up. Keep moving. Don't look back. Although that later scene on the subway – when Mercy and Swan are sitting there across from the prom couples – as JB Smoove would say, "That was some poignant shit right there."

I mentioned that Walter Hill worked production on *Bullit*. So how do you think Steve McQueen would've responded if this greenhorn 2nd assistant director came up to him and said, "Hey, Steve, I've got this great script you should read?" Wait a minute, maybe Walter did do that. Because three years later, *The Getaway* was released – directed by Sam Peckinpah, starring Steve McQueen, and written by Walter Hill. Jeez...

If you go back and look closely at the car explosion scene and see that Orphan flying through the frame – that's Konrad Sheehan (the Skate Punk) and that was no ratchet gag.

There's been some terrific television made over these last years. If you're interested in movie production, check out *The Offer*. It's a limited series about the making of *The Godfather*. It's a realistic journey inside the process. So, here's another idea – hey, Paramount – yeah I'm talkin' to you – how about Paramount+ turning *Purple Fury* into a limited series? Just like *The Offer*, only more limited.

54

I said maybe I had another story about William Friedkin in me. But nah – the moon ain't right, the tide's up, and I quit drinking. Besides, Friedkin just died and he's probably down there conspiring with Lucifer about how they're gonna prank Bobby Knight when he shows up.

55

I mentioned I had a couple of icing stories. Yeah, okay.

Baseball is the cruelest game. Ty Cobb was a mean sonofabitch. And Tommy Lee Jones was typecast in Ron Shelton's *Cobb*.

I signed on to handle the baseball in *Cobb*. It was more administrative than anything – making sure the right players were in the right place at the right time. Shelton would handle the baseball – he played the game. He knew the game.

We're still in prep – working out of Ron's office in Hollywood – Crossroads of the World on Sunset Blvd. It's been a long, typical day for me – tracking down players, tracking down a double for Tommy Lee Jones. Tracking down a practice field where this double could demonstrate some sliding techniques for said Mr. Jones.

I've been on my feet for hours and I'm beat, but it's all set up, so I schlepp back to the office and check in – Ron's not back yet – and I lie down on a couch in the waiting room and put my feet up. Two minutes later, the door bangs open – it's Shelton, followed by Tommy Lee Jones – who immediately starts shouting at me –

"Wake up, man! Look inspired! Hey, Ron, I thought we were making a movie here!"

Oh jeez. Okay. That's the way it's gonna be.

We head down to Poinsettia Park where there's an empty, beat-up baseball field. The double I found is waiting – young guy, good athlete, played at Cal State Fullerton I think, and when he and Tommy Lee Jones stand side by side for Polaroids, the body types are damn close – except for Mr. Jones' head which is unusually large.

Then, on that hard-packed base path, this double demonstrates slide after slide. Shelton talking him through the variations, Jones observing intently. The best actors, especially when they're stepping out of their comfort zones – really pay attention.

The double sucks it up – because hitting that crushed granite again and again is no picnic. Finally, he demonstrates the last slide and we're done at Poinsettia Park. There's a couple more weeks until commencement of principal photography. Tommy Lee Jones is headed back to his ranch in Texas while I'm off to Detroit to pull together two full teams of players and personnel and keep them in a holding pattern until the schedule gets finalized.

As we say our goodbyes, Tommy Lee Jones announces he's gonna practice sliding back on his ranch.

Shelton says great.

And I say, "You know, hitting the ground like that, you want to be careful."

"Son, don't tell me how to be."

I go stone cold. I mean, I'm a grown man here – I've got a wife and kid, I've got some miles of my own on me. So, yeah, I right then and there turn down the thermostat and decide to keep it near freezing the rest of the movie.

Detroit goes fine. After a few days, I've got two dozen credible baseball guys – all sorted out, and good to go. I'm about to fly back to L.A. when I get a call from the production office – Tommy Lee Jones just broke an ankle practicing sliding back on his ranch in Texas.

The whole schedule gets shoved into the future, Detroit is shit-canned entirely, and Mr. Jones shoots the movie hiding a limp.

So yeah, put some ice on it.

56

Icing is meant for professional purposes only. Do not try this at home. I'm serious – it creates a very potent vibration. Putting it out there can do real harm, especially to children. Spouses too. So, use it sparingly, and only at work.

Or maybe online. Yeah, I guess in certain interwebian situations it can be the best response. Because going negative online is a lost cause – any disagreement quickly devolving into more and more inventive ways that somebody should go fuck themselves. Plus, engaging in online snarkiness will chip away at your soul in ways you don't even realize. Even reading that shit's a mistake.

Instead, feel free to make like Casper. Or Frosty. It's really the easiest way to settle things. Or if you have to, I suppose you can go that passive-aggressive route – you know – kill 'em with kindness. But only if you're not in a hurry. In the words of a wise man -

"This 'killing them with kindness' is taking way longer than I expected."

57

Shaquille O'Neal has always been a huge fan of *The Warriors*. Huge. As we learned when he won his first championship with the Lakers then took to the stage shouting, "Can you dig it?! Can you dig it?!" over and over.

I wish I had known that back in 1993 when we worked together on *Blue Chips*. (Though Shaq was just 6 years old when *The Warriors* came out, so who knows when he first saw it.) I certainly didn't know he was such a fan, or he would have learned I played a Baseball Fury. It might have helped. He and I got along fine at first. I met him during prep down in the gym at Loyola Marymount University. We were running scrimmages with the most talented group of basketball players ever assembled for a movie. I actually jumped into a game for a few possessions – it was a trip, man, it was fast – these guys were not only big, they were freaking fast. I even drew a charge from Shaq in the open court – probably the most dangerous stunt of my life. And like I said, we got along fine.

Then we got to Indiana. Maybe it was the Bobby Knight vibe, or maybe it was Shaq seeing how Billy Friedkin was turning sour on me. But for some reason, Shaquille O'Neal chose to diss me – by not shaking my hand when I offered it – right in front of a bunch of people I respected and had to work with – Bob Cousy, Dick Vitale, Rick Pitino, Nick Nolte.

So, I went into ice mode. And kept it chilly for day after day as we set up and shot all those basketball games. And it got to him – this 20-year-old, newly minted millionaire – me icing him like that. It got under his skin. And I admit to taking some grim satisfaction in not responding to the overtures he began putting out as he tried to break the ice.

Three days into this deep freeze, I'm in the locker room, making sure the next teams of players are sorted out and good to go, when I suddenly feel this gigantic presence behind me, and then these humongous black arms wrap around my chest and I'm being lifted off my feet and suspended in mid-air by Shaquille O'Neal who waves me around like a rag doll in front of all the players, shouting my name over and over again, "Rob Ryder! Rob Ryder!" Squeezing me until I'm gasping for breath, feeling my ribs about to crack, thinking – Okay, so there are weirder ways to die in this world, but at the moment, I can't think of one.

Until I finally save myself. The only way I know how – by melting into the arms of Shaquille O'Neal.

And Shaq and I get along fine after that.

58

Okay, I have a confession to make. That crazy movie idea I came up with about all the old Warriors pressed into action at a fan convention? Well, I wrote the screenplay. That's why this damn book has taken so long. But I got it done – *The Warlords* – a lean mean 104 pages. Then I rewrote it. Then again. And now it's good to go. What future does it face? We'll find out. I'll keep you posted.

59

I don't like it when books are cluttered up with introductions and tables of contents, acknowledgements and indexes, so I'm gonna sneak this in here.

Thanks to Gloria Gocheva, the talented Bulgarian, who put together the cover art. And thanks to Tessy Ogidi in Nigeria for finessing the formatting.

Thanks to my beta readers – Mark Rogers, David Blinder, Isabella Barbara, Randolph Runsafter, David Williams, Miriam Castillo, Ted Williams, Lilly Pinero, Chris Piaggio and Jessica Alexandria.

Thanks and a tip of the hat to Shaun Powers and Jason Maher for not only reading but for helping me get my facts straight.

Thanks to my love, Pamela Fletcher, for sharing this foxhole with me – keeping the powder dry and the vibration high.

Thanks to all the promoters for putting on these Fan-Cons. As someone coming from movie production, I truly appreciate what goes into what you pull off, year after year. Talk about getting pecked to death by ducks…

Thanks to *The Warriors*' Cast and Crew. Every last one of them (and that's a lot of talent there). Thanks for powering this iconic cult classic straight through to completion way back when. And who knew? Who knew.

Lastly, thanks to all the fans, everywhere. And here I can get emotional, so I'll just say this - May you all live long, healthy, prosperous lives, filled with peace and love. Take care of yourselves. And each other.

60

There's an unspoken rule among stuntmen – never let 'em know you're hurt.

We're back on the subway bathroom set at Astoria Studio. Day after day, cast and crew, moving in rhythm as one of the great movie fights is filmed in 35-millimeter Technicolor.

Baxley's really got his shit together – as does the DP, Andy Laszlo. And all the guys, the Warriors, the Punks, and Deborah, systematically working our way through dozens and dozens of pieces of action. Jery Hewitt's spreading his good-natured magic – he's even got A.J. Bakunas with the program, putting in some solid work.

Walter's a confident director. By this point in the schedule, he knows he's got a movie here – seeing the trees and the forest – the whole damn thing.

I know I'm in for some hard knocks in this brawl, but I'm like, bring it on. 'Cause you know what? – I get to throw Vermin into the mirrors. Finally, a little retribution.

As we move through the days, we learn to be ready, even when we're not in front of the cameras. Because it's a complicated piece, and each set-up has to be looked at from every angle. So, Swan's getting wailed on by Bakunas – just the two of them, right? But who's in the background – who's gonna show up in the wide angle shot?

So yeah, we're ready, we're primed. There's no hitting the doughnuts because you can hear your name called at any moment. Besides, it's a fucking thrill – watching it come together. Rooting for each other. Everybody getting along.

I take some real shots, but I feel like I've gotten the hang of it – doing that quick twitch thing to sell the punch, the kick. When Cochise slams the stall door into me, I let it hit me full force – knowing the more area of my body it hits, the easier the blow will be. Spread the pain. Then I have to fall backwards and hit the floor, telling myself, it's cool, it's cool, just don't hit the back of your head, and I don't.

Then, as I'm getting up, Cochise nails me with a right cross to my jaw. No contact. David Harris is a fine actor and an excellent athlete – his punch just misses my chin, and I sell it with a snap of my head. Baxley's happy so we move on. And now Mercy's really going to town – Deborah Van Valkenburgh doing some excellent physical work – jumping on Gary Baxley's back, biting his shoulder, getting thrown off.

And Marcelino Sanchez – Rembrandt – spraying red paint into Skate Punk's face and nailing him with a right cross. Konrad Sheehan takes it like a man. As does Marcelino later in the scene when he takes a punch to the nuts and a left hook to the head.

So many pieces of action – dozens and dozens – that when finally assembled by the editors will run barely two minutes in length.

Now it's my turn again, getting rushed by Snow, a bat in his hands. Brian Tyler's the Warrior who left the movie business to become a New York State Trooper. He's the biggest of the Warriors – tall and solidly built. And just like Snow, Brian Tyler doesn't have much to say. He just gets the job done. So yeah, here I am again, taking a bat to the ribs. After each take he asks me, "You good? That too hard?"

"I'm good, man. I'm good."

And I am, because Vermin is about to have his blind date with the mirrors.

Terry Michos is not a small man. 5'11, 165 pounds. All muscle. By now he's really found his voice in this movie – providing some comic relief (remember, kids, Vermin's got the big one).

But he's got nothing to say here. In fact, the entire bathroom brawl is shot without a line of dialogue.

Craig Baxley maps out the action for Michos and me – referring to his shot list, schematics. We'll be shooting it in two parts – Vermin finishes taking out Jery Hewitt when I rush him, grab his left shoulder, and spin him around, throwing a looping right uppercut into his gut, doubling him up. Then I reach for his neck with my left hand, grab him through the crotch with my right, lift him off the floor and…and…

And that's where we'll cut and reset the camera angles. Because you don't want to send one of the stars of the movie crashing into some mirror and ending up in the hospital when you still need him for the last scene on the beach. So, Craig Baxley's brought his cousin Gary in from Hollywood to double Michos for the actual contact.

It seems like a straightforward stunt – you see this shit all the time in the movies. But when you're there on the set, you realize just how hairy even the simplest gag can be. What part of his body's gonna smash into the mirrors? And more importantly, how's he gonna fall onto the sinks before he hits the floor? Those mirrors might be candy glass, engineered to break without slicing anyone up, but the sinks are hard ceramic – the real deal – and Vermin's gonna be falling right on them.

Terry Michos and I rehearse the first shot at half-speed. The punch to the gut, the crotch grab. I see Baxley conferring with Walter. They want me to lift Vermin off the floor and start to throw him – and that's where they'll cut, and Michos won't go flying anywhere.

Walter says, "All right, let's see another rehearsal, full speed."

So we take our positions, Baxley nods at Walter and says, "Action." And we go into it – the shoulder grab, the spin, the punch, the crotch grab, but as I go to lift Terry Michos, I realize, man, this dude's a fucking load. I mean, I can lift him into the air, but throwing him…Jeez. And Gary Baxley's built even bigger than Michos, so how's that gonna work?

I hear Walter scoff. Craig Baxley walks up to me, looks me up and down, and squeezes my right bicep like, I thought you were strong. I say nothing, but this is like someone saying to you – "Yo, pick up that couch and throw it through the window." In other words, it ain't happening, and we all know it.

Baxley smiles – have he and Walter been fucking with me? He turns to one of the prop guys, or is it a grip? "Bring in the mini-tramp."

And that's how we do the stunt – picking up the second piece of the action with Gary Baxley doubling Vermin – me grabbing him through the crotch and bouncing him off this mini-trampoline which remains just out of frame – as I fling him through the air and into the mirrors.

It's a gas – me finally getting some shots in after spending the whole movie on the receiving end of bats, fists, elbows, knees, tiled walls, and bathroom doors.

Gary Baxley does a great job – getting those mirrors to shatter the way they do – the back of his head smashing the first mirror, his butt and feet demolishing the second. And I see that he's breaking his fall onto the sinks with his right hand – but still, his knees hit the sinks hard, and that shit's gotta hurt. But no one would ever know.

We're almost done. My time on *The Warriors* finally coming to an end. There's one more stunt to do. In this last piece, I rush Swan, he throws a right hook into my ribs, and I fold over. Then, as I'm straightening up, Swan throws a knee into my face, and it's lights out for this Punk as I smash into the wall and crumple to the floor.

So, we shoot this gag. Then shoot it again. And I swear Walter's having way too much fun watching Michael Beck beat me up this one last time. After the third take, I've had enough. I don't care how many stunt adjustments I'm getting, how much overtime I'm racking up. I am done. I am beat. But here we go again.

This next take, Swan's knee catches me hard, just under the chin, and I smash into the tile wall harder than ever. When I hit the floor, I just lie there. I hear a far-off voice say, "Cut." I'm motionless, the wind knocked out of me. My head throbs and I'm seeing those little sparkling drops of light that aren't supposed to be there. So I just lie on the floor. Trying to pull myself together.

It's a truly existential moment. Eyes glazed over, fantasizing about how instead of this, I could've been a pro hooper in Lapland right now – in bed with a beautiful Finnish girl, naked under a giant goose-down comforter, wood fire burning, brandy flowing, two reindeer waiting patiently outside in the snow, hitched to our sleigh.

But no – when I reached that proverbial fork in the road, I chose the movie business. And here I am, splayed out on the floor of a fake subway bathroom in Queens, trying to convince myself that that stabbing pain in my lungs isn't a giant sliver of broken rib.

Out of the corner of my eye I see the camera crew reloading the cameras. No one's paying me any attention. Until I spot the kindly DP, Andy Laszlo, noticing me lying there motionless. Laszlo nods to Walter who glances at me then turns to Baxley and says, "Hey, Bax."

I close my eyes a second, trying to suck it up. Get some air into my lungs, get the ringing out of my ears. Then Baxley's there, taking a knee, hunching over me.

"You okay?" he asks.

"I, uh…yeah. I just need a sec…"

"But you're all right?"

"Yeah. Yeah, I'm all right."

"Then get the fuck up, we're going again."

The End

Milton Keynes UK
Ingram Content Group UK Ltd.
UKHW021834060724
445042UK00014BA/763